TECH TALK

Pre-Intermediate Student's Book

Vicki Hollett & John Sydes

OXFORD

UNIVERSITY PRESS

CONTENTS

1 *What's the job?*

Jobs

1 Read about some different jobs. Are any similar to yours? (How?)

ARCHITECT

- Works for a construction company.
- Designs buildings, produces plans, specifications, and drawings.
- Negotiates with builders and inspects construction work.

FIELD SERVICE ENGINEER

- Works for an office equipment manufacturer.
- Visits customers' sites and repairs and maintains machines.
- Spends a lot of time driving from place to place.

HELP DESK TECHNICIAN

- Works for a credit card company.
- Provides technical support.
- Solves customers' problems over the phone.
- Works night shifts.

SOFTWARE ENGINEER

- Works for a bank.
- Writes, tests, and debugs code.
- Updates security features and troubleshoots.
- Is responsible for a project team.

WAREHOUSE MANAGER

- Works for a paper company.
- Receives shipments and checks quantities.
- Keeps records of inventory.
- Manages a database.

QUALITY CONTROLLER

- Works for a pharmaceutical company.
- Collects and examines product samples.
- Analyses data and writes reports.

2 Look at the words in blue in the text. Find the word which means:

1 bargains, reaches agreement by discussion
2 parts of the working day
3 puts in the latest information
4 stocks of goods and materials
5 goods that are transported
6 finds and corrects faults and problems
7 keeps in good working order
8 specimens, small quantities of a product that show what the rest is like
9 looks at something closely to make sure it's OK
10 examines something carefully to understand and explain it.

3 In your opinion, which of these people:

1 travel the most and the least?
2 use computers the most?
3 work the longest hours?
4 don't need to wear special clothing?
5 sometimes work outside?
6 meet lots of different people?
7 need the most qualifications?
8 make the most money?
9 have the best and the worst jobs? (Why?)

4 Look back at the job descriptions in **1** and match the verbs and nouns that go together.

Verbs (actions)	Nouns (things)
1 to work for	a records
2 to work	b time
3 to keep	c code
4 to be responsible for	d a bank
5 to spend	e support
6 to solve	f night shifts
7 to debug	g problems
8 to provide	h a project team

5 What do you do at work? Write some sentences describing your job and read them to the class.

Example
I work for …
I'm responsible for …
I spend a lot of time …
I …

6 Work with a partner. Take turns to describe the jobs of people you know, for example, your boss, your husband / wife, your brother / sister, etc.

Example
A *What does your wife do?*
B *She's a laboratory technician. She works at a chemical company. She tests and analyses samples. She …*

Present Simple

Add *s* to the verb with *he*, *she*, or *it*.
I work for a bank. She works for a bank.
Use *do* or *does* to make questions.
Do *you work night shifts?*
Does *he work night shifts?*

7 Play a game with the class. One person thinks of a job. (It can be any job, for example, astronaut, truck driver, tax collector.) The others have to work out what the job is. They can only ask questions where the answer is *yes* or *no*.

Example
Do you travel a lot?
Do you use a computer?
Do you work long hours?
Do you need to wear special clothing?
Do you work outside?
Do you meet a lot of different people?
Do you need qualifications to do your job?
Do you make a lot of money?

Coming and going

a

b

c

d

e

1 What do you think the people in the pictures above are saying? Listen to some conversations.

   1 Match each one to the correct picture.
   2 Say if the people are arriving or leaving.

2 Listen to conversation 1 again.

   1 Was the meeting successful? What do they say about it?
   2 What do they say *Thank you* for?

3 Listen to conversation 2 again and complete the questions.

   1 Did you have .... finding us?
   2 .... a cup of coffee first?

Think of more questions to ask a visitor about their journey.
Think of more things to offer a visitor.

4 Listen to conversation 3 again.

   1 Where's the woman's passport?
   2 What other ID does she have?
   3 What does she need to do?

What do visitors to your company need to do to pass through security?

5 Here is conversation 4, but it's in the wrong order. Number the sentences. Then listen again and check your answers.

☐ You're welcome.

☐ Do you want me to give you a lift?

1 Can I use your phone?

☐ I just need to call a taxi.

☐ Where are you going? To the station?

☐ Yes, go ahead.

☐ Yes.

☐ Could you? That's very kind of you.

6 Listen to conversation 5 again.

   1 What does he need to do to enter?
   2 Where's the office?
   3 How does he ask for help? Complete the sentences.

I'm .... I have three big boxes to .... up.
Can somebody .... me a ....?

7 Complete some more conversations using phrases from the list.

Would you like	Could you
of course	Can I
Do you want a hand	I'm afraid
No, it's all right, thanks	I can manage
Do you want me to	please

1 A .... hold this cable for me?
  B Yes, ...

2 A .... with your bags?
  B Yes, ...

3 A .... use your fax?
  B .... it's broken.

4 A .... call a taxi for you?
  B .... I'll catch the bus.

5 A .... some help?
  B Thanks, but I think ....

8 Work with a partner. Act out these situations.

	A	B
1	Ask **B** to help you carry some boxes up to the fourth floor.	Say yes.
2	Ask **B** if you can leave your laptop in their office.	Say no and give a reason.
3	You need to borrow a car this weekend. Ask **B** for theirs.	Say no and give a reason.
4	Tell **B** about a job you need to do this week.	Offer to help.
5	Tell **B** you need to go to the airport.	Offer to give **A** a lift.

9 Work with a partner. Take turns making a visitor welcome. Act out short conversations.

1 Greet your visitor when they arrive. Help them pass through security.
2 Find out if they would like coffee or something to eat.
3 Introduce them to your boss or another member of your team.
4 Offer to show them around your workplace.
5 It's time for them to leave. Find out if they need a taxi. Say goodbye.

10 Decide which replies are OK. (Sometimes more than one is possible.)

1 It's great to see you again!
  a It's great to see you, too.
  b Nice to meet you.
  c Thank you.

2 Thanks, that's very kind of you.
  a Not at all.
  b Please.
  c You're welcome.

3 I'd love a cup of coffee.
  a I get you one.
  b I'll get you one.
  c I'm afraid I only have tea.

4 How are you doing?
  a Not too bad, thanks. And you?
  b Fine, thanks. I've nearly finished.
  c I'm painting the garage door.

5 Oops! I'm sorry!
  a That's OK.
  b You're welcome.
  c No problem.

6 Is this your screwdriver?
  a Yes, it is.
  b Yes, of course.
  c Yes, do you want to borrow it?

7 Can I borrow your torch?
  a Yes, go ahead.
  b Yes, help yourself.
  c Yes, I can borrow it to you.

8 What do you do?
  a How do you do?
  b I'm in computers.
  c I'm replacing the disk drive.

9 I'll be getting along then.
  a Go ahead.
  b It was nice meeting you.
  c Thank you for coming.

10 Thanks for showing me around the plant.
  a Goodbye.
  b It was a pleasure.
  c It doesn't matter.

2 Is that correct?

Spelling things out

1 Do you have to speak English on the phone? (Who to and what about?)

2 (2.1) Listen to a phone call and check this email address. If it's wrong, correct it.

g_barlow@bqe.com

3 (2.1) Listen again and complete the sentences.

1 It's very noisy here. Can you ....?
2 Are you ....?
3 No. Just a ...., I need to open a file.
4 OK, go ....
5 .... you spell that?
6 .... g dot bahlow at VQE dot com, ...?
7 You're welcome. Anything ....?
8 No, ..., thanks.

4 Here are some similar phrases. Match each one to a phrase in **3**.

a Can you spell that for me?
b Is that everything?
c Hang on.
d Shall I start?
e No, there's nothing else.
f I'm afraid I can't hear you.
g Let me read that back to you. It's …
h I'm ready now.

5 The English alphabet has seven sounds. Put the letters in the correct columns. Then spell your name and your company name aloud.

D	E	G	J	K	N	O	P	R
S	T	U	V	W	X	Y		

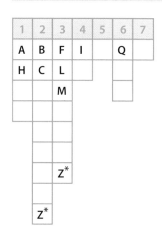

1	2	3	4	5	6	7
A	B	F	I		Q	
H	C	L				
		M				
		Z*				
Z*						

z is pronounced /zed/ **BrE** – z is pronounced /ziː/ **AmE**

6 Label the parts of these addresses with words from the list.

| hyphen |
| underscore |
| dot |
| at |
| colon |
| slash* |

A_Shaper-78@ringtip.net

ftp://www.oup.com/elt/gb/

We also say 'back slash'.

Dictate some email and website addresses that you know to the class. They should write them down.

7 Work with a partner and act out some calls.

A – look at file 28 on page 111.
B – look at file 1 on page 102.

Measurements

1 Do you know any non-metric measurements?

  1 Which is longer: a kilometre or a mile?
  2 Which is bigger: a litre or a gallon?

🎧 Listen and check your answers. Write down the numbers you hear.

2 Read the measurements in the table aloud. Check the notes on decimal numbers for help.

1 mile = 1.609 km	1 inch = 25.4 mm
1 gallon = 4.54609 L	1 pound = 0.45 kg

3 Work with a partner or in small groups and do the quiz. Make a note of your answers.

Measurements quiz

  1 Which is longer: a centimetre or an inch?

  2 Which is shorter: a metre or a yard?

  3 Which is taller: a 200-metre building or a 200-foot building?

  4 Which is faster: 100 kilometres an hour or 100 miles an hour?

  5 Which is hotter: 100 degrees Celsius or 100 degrees Fahrenheit?

  6 Which is colder: 0 degrees Celsius or 0 degrees Fahrenheit?

  7 Which is heavier: a kilogram or a pound?

  8 Which is lighter: a gram or an ounce?

  9 Which holds more water: a one-litre bottle or a one-pint bottle?

10 Which is heavier: a two-tonne truck or a two-ton truck?

See file 8 on page 104 for answers.

Decimal numbers

Write decimal points as a point (.), not a comma (,).

After the point, say numbers separately.
1.609   *One point six oh nine*

Before the point, say numbers together.
25.4   *Twenty five point four*

After the point, 0 is *zero* or *oh*.
4.54609   *Four point five four six oh nine*

Before the point, 0 is *nought*, or *zero*, or we don't pronounce it at all.
0.45   *nought point four five* or *point four five*

4 Match these abbreviations to the correct measurements in the quiz.

°C	km	in	yd	L	oz	cm
gal	m	mph	°F	lb	ft	

5 Work with a partner.

A – look at the information below.
B – look at file 13 on page 105.

A
Ask your partner questions. Complete the chart.

Example *How many yards is one metre?*

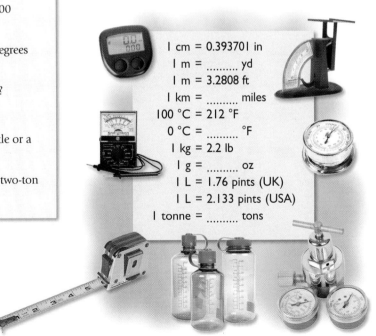

1 cm = 0.39370I in
1 m = ... yd
1 m = 3.2808 ft
1 km = ... miles
100 °C = 2I2 °F
0 °C = ... °F
1 kg = 2.2 lb
1 g = ... oz
1 L = I.76 pints (UK)
1 L = 2.133 pints (USA)
1 tonne = ... tons

Defects

1 What different parts does this clock have? Label it with the words and phrases in the list.

numbers	base	alarm
hour hand	face	minute hand

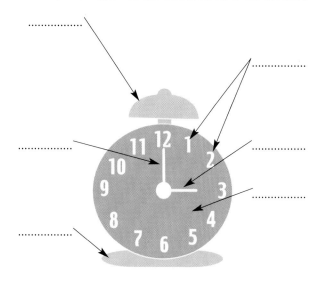

2 Look at some more clocks and listen to a phone call.

1 Which clock is it about?
2 What's wrong with it?
3 What are they going to do about it?

3 Listen again and complete the sentences.

1 Hi, Franz, ...?
2 The .... is the wrong ....
3 Yes, the .... five centimetres and it's eight.
4 It .... our packaging.
5 Send it ...., Franz, and I'll give you a ....

4 Look at all the other clocks and say what's wrong with them.

5 Match these defects to the correct clock.

1 It doesn't have an alarm.
2 There are no hands.
3 It's too small.
4 The alarm is in the wrong place.
5 The numbers are upside down.
6 It has too many hands.
7 It's the wrong shape.
8 The base is missing.
9 It only has one hand.
10 The alarm is the wrong colour.
11 The base is the wrong size. It's too big.
12 There are two hour hands and there's no minute hand.
13 The hands are too long. They don't fit inside the case.
14 The numbers are the wrong way round. They're back to front.

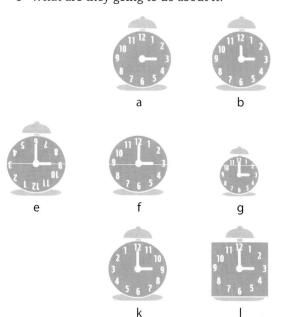

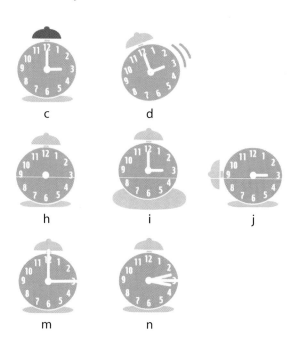

6 Use words from the list to label the pictures.

hand cart	cork	handle	title
receiver	spout	tights*	
traffic lights*	wheels	blades	

tights **BrE** – pantyhose **AmE**
traffic lights **BrE** – traffic signals **AmE**

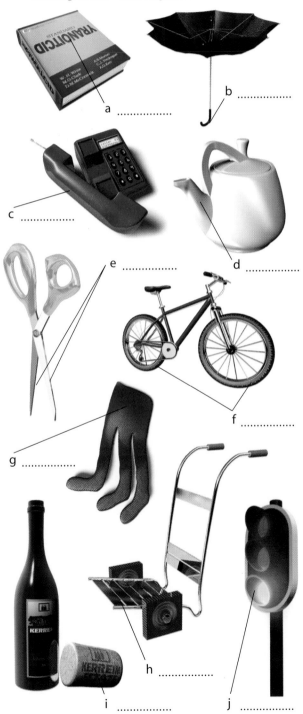

a ....

b ....

c ....

e ....

d ....

f ....

g ....

h ....

i ....

j ....

7 Describe what's wrong. Use phrases from the box.

It doesn't have ...
The ... is / are missing.
There is / are no ...
There is / are too many ...
The ... doesn't fit
The .... is / are   in the wrong place.
                 too ...
                 back to front.
                 upside down.
                 inside out.
                 the wrong shape /
                   colour / size.

8 Work with a partner.

A – look at the information below.
B – look at file 33 on page 114.

A
Call 1
You know there were some quality problems at your factory last week. You sold your partner this filing cabinet. They call you to complain.
1 Find out what's wrong with it.
2 Make notes to give to your quality department.

Call 2
You bought this printer cable, ink cartridge, and web cam from your partner last week. There are some problems with them. Call your partner and explain what's wrong.

You ordered 3 metres

2 metres

Wrong shape for your printer

Missing base

3 What are the numbers?

Project planning

1 (3.1) Listen to some people planning a job. Make a list of the things they'll need. What job is it?

Packing materials:

Time:

Vehicles and manpower:

Money:

---

will / won't

We use *will* to give and ask for information about the future, and to offer help.
*How many boxes **will** we need? The materials **will** be $2,400. I'll send you some bubble wrap.*

With words like *I, you, we,* etc. use the contracted form, *'ll*. Will not = *won't*.

*It'll be $5,400. We'll do the packing. It **won't** fit into one truck.*

---

2 Turn to page 120 and read the conversation with a partner. Remember to use the contracted forms of *will*.

3 The speakers made a lot of estimates in the conversation. Complete the words below.

1 B How many boxes will we need?
   A It's hard to say e..........:
   B R.......... speaking?
   A A.......... three hundred.

2 A How far is your new office?
   B A.......... ten miles.

3 A Eight men and two trucks for one day ... You're l......... at s.......... l.......... three thousand dollars.

4 B So in total, it'll be $5,400?
   A Yes, a..........:

(3.1) Now listen and check.

4 Practise making some estimates. Roughly speaking:

1 how far is it from your home to your workplace?
2 how long does it take you to get to work?
3 how far will you travel this week?
4 how much will you spend on petrol this month?
5 how much will you spend on travelling this year (cars, petrol, flights, trains, etc.)?

Countable and uncountable nouns

English nouns can be countable or uncountable.
*How many **boxes** will we need?*
*How much **bubble wrap** will we need?*

Countable nouns have a plural form.
*box, **boxes**, truck, **trucks**, man, **men***

Uncountable nouns are always singular.
equipment, ~~equipments~~, money, ~~moneys~~

Uncountable nouns take a singular verb form.
The packaging costs a lot.
*Some of our equipment **is** fragile.*

---

5 Are these nouns countable [C] or uncountable [U]?

1	equipment	7	fact	13	defect	19	experiment
2	computer	8	news	14	waste	20	test
3	machine	9	information	15	pollution	21	physics
4	machinery	10	data	16	petrol*	22	money
5	packaging	11	advice	17	gas	23	dollar
6	pack	12	suggestion	18	research	24	time

petrol **BrE** – gas or gasoline **AmE**

6 Tick (✓) the sentences that are correct. Correct the sentences that are wrong.

Example

much
How ~~many~~ time will we need?

1 I need some informations about train times.

2 How many times a year should we replace these filters?

3 There are a lot of datas here that we don't need.

4 How much new machines will you need next year?

5 All our machinery are state of the art.

6 These equipment is very difficult to use.

7 If the tests is successful, we'll start production in about six weeks.

8 Physics is the study of matter and energy.

9 How much dollars do we need?

10 The goal is zero defects and zero wastes.

7 Work in teams. Teams should sit in different parts of the room, if possible, so you can't hear what other teams are saying. Each team will plan a different job.

Discuss what you need to do for your job. Write a list of the equipment and manpower you will need, and estimate how long it will take, and how much it will cost. When you have finished, present your lists to the other teams. They will guess what the job is.

Team 1 – look at file 6 on page 103.
Team 2 – look at file 12 on page 105.
Team 3 – look at file 17 on page 107.
Team 4 – look at file 30 on page 112.

Making comparisons

1 🎧 What's special about these three vehicles? What unusual things do you think they can do? Listen to an advertisement for a radio programme about them and find out if you're right.

THE CARVER
Price: €42,000
Top speed: 180 km/h
Dimensions: 340 x 130 x 140 cm (L,W,H)*
Weight: 620 kg
Engine output: kW/hp 48.5/65
Max range: 630 km

THE SEGWAY HT™
Price: €5,500
Top speed: 20 km/h
Dimensions: 48 x 64 x variable (L,W,H)*
Weight: 43 kg
Engine output: kW/hp 1.5/2.0
Max range: 19 km

THE SKYCAR
Price: approx €2m
Top speed: 630 km/h
Dimensions: 5.5 x 2.7 x 1.8 m (L,W,H)*
Weight: 1,000 kg
Engine output: kW/hp 716/960
Max range: 1,450 km

*(L, W, H) = Length, Width, Height

2 (3.2) Listen again and answer the questions.

1 What's the subject of tonight's *Car Chat* show?
2 Why does Peter think the Segway HT is 'the coolest thing'?
3 How does it compare to a car and a bike?
4 What happens to the Carver when it goes round a bend?
5 How does it compare to a normal car?
6 What's the worst thing about driving?
7 How does a Skycar compare to a normal car?

Comparing two things

With short adjectives, use -*er* (+ *than*).
It's *faster* **than** *a normal car*.
With long adjectives, use *more / less* (+ *than*).
It's **more** *exciting* **than** *a car and it's* **less** *noisy*.
Irregular forms: *good*   It's **better**.
             bad   It's **worse**.
             far   It goes **further**.
Or use *as … as*.
It isn't **as** *cheap* **as** *a car*.

3 Look at the specifications for the vehicles in **1**. How do they compare to other vehicles like cars, bicycles, and motorbikes? Make more sentences using the patterns in the box above.

Example
The Segway HT isn't as expensive as a car but it's slower.
It's taller than a bicycle and it's much heavier.

Comparing three or more things

With short adjectives, use (*the*) -*est*.
With long adjectives, use (*the*) *most / least*.
The Skycar is **the** *fastest vehicle and it's also*
the most *expensive*.
Irregular forms: *good*   It's **the best**.
             bad   It's **the worst**.
             far   It goes **the furthest**.

4 Now compare the three vehicles. In your opinion, which one is:

1 the most useful in a city?
2 the easiest to use?
3 the most difficult to maintain?
4 the safest?
5 the least comfortable to travel in or on?
6 the most fun*?
7 the most exciting?
8 the best vehicle for you to use to get to work?

Compare your answers with some other students and see if you agree.

Fun means enjoyable. For example, *The boat trip was fun*.
Funny describes something strange or something that makes you laugh. For example, *The machine is making a funny noise. It was the funniest movie I've ever seen. We all laughed.*

5 Hold a competition with the class.

1 Brainstorm twelve different things you can use to get from one place to another. Write them on the board.

Example
bicycle, hot air balloon, donkey

2 Take turns choosing two different things and comparing them.

Example
car / bicycle – A car is noisier than a bicycle.

Write the adjectives you use on the board too. Nobody can use the same adjective twice. The person who makes the last sentence is the winner.

3 Look at the list of adjectives and make more sentences about the vehicles. Say which is the *fastest, slowest, noisiest*, etc.

Example *A plane is the fastest.*

6 Work in groups. You need to go to a conference in New York. What is:

1 the fastest way to get there?
2 the cheapest way to get there?
3 the best way to get there?

Compare your answers with the class.

Comparisons

1 Look at the two drink cans. What do you think they are made of? Which one do you think is:

1 stronger?
2 more environmentally friendly?
3 better?

Dr Freeman works for Scientific Generics, Cambridge, England, and he's invented a really useful can for fizzy drinks. Instead of aluminium, his can is made of four layers of paper and amazingly, it can withstand pressures of five atmospheres – twice the pressure of traditional aluminium cans. The paper cans are also easier to recycle and cause far less pollution.

Short adjectives – add *-er*.
It's *stronger / safer / cheaper* ...

Long adjectives – use *more / less*.
It's **more** *environmentally friendly*.
It's **less** *expensive*.

Adjectives ending in -y – change -y to -i and add *-er*.
easy → *easier*

2 Complete these sentences. Use comparative forms of the adjectives in the list.

comfortable	noisy	safe	~~easy~~
interesting	cheap	slow	useful
sophisticated	heavy		

1 That can opener is difficult to use. Try this one. It's *easier*.
2 I'm afraid it's too expensive. Do you have a .... model?
3 Those sensors are very basic, but these ones are ....
4 Motorbikes are dangerous. A car is much ....
5 Put your ear protectors on. This workshop is much .... than the last one.
6 The last training course was very boring. I hope this one is ....
7 My back hurts. I think I need a .... chair.
8 You have a fast Internet connection. Mine is ....
9 This hammer is too light. We need a .... one.
10 Which is .... when you're travelling: a computer or a mobile phone?

Numbers

1 Find the number of:

1	cents in a dollar	11
2	days in January	50
3	hours in a day	206
4	seconds in a minute	9
5	legs on a spider	90
6	letters in the English alphabet	24
7	months in a year	60
8	planets in our solar system	64
9	states in the USA	365
10	weeks in a year / cards in a pack	100
11	keys on a piano	52
12	sides on a triangle	26
13	degrees in a right angle	3
14	players in a football team	31
15	squares on a chess board	8
16	holes on a golf course	18
17	bones in the human body	88
18	minutes in a quarter of an hour	12
19	days in a year.	15

2 Work with a partner and check your answers.

Example
A _How many cents are there in a dollar?_
B _A hundred. How many … are there …?_

What's missing?

Work with a partner. Say what's missing.

a 10, 100, ..., 10,000, 100,000, ...
b the day before yesterday, yesterday, ...,
   tomorrow, ...
c ...., child, teenager, ..., old person
d M, T, ..., T, F, S, ...
e red, ..., yellow, ..., blue, dark blue,
   purple
f J, ..., M, A, M, J, ..., ..., S, ..., N, D
g Q W E ...... T ...... U I O P
h 1, ..., 9, 16, 25, ..., 49, 64, 81,100
i the Sun, Mercury, ..., the Earth, Mars,
   Jupiter, Saturn, Uranus, ..., Pluto
   (Hint: My very excellent mother just sent us
            nine pizzas.)

Telephoning

1 When might you need to say these things?

1 Can you speak up?
2 Can you hold on a second?
3 I need to go. Can we talk again later?
4 Is this a good time to call?
5 You're breaking up.
6 Anyway …

Can you speak up? – when someone is speaking too quietly

2 Match these situations to the correct phrase.

a You want someone to wait.
b The reception is bad.
c Someone is speaking too quietly.
d You think someone you're calling might
   be busy.
e You're planning to finish the call.
f You need to end the call because you're in
   a hurry.

4 How does it work?

Gadgets

1 What James Bond movies do you know? Do you remember any of the gadgets? What special features do James Bond's watches have? What do they enable him to do?

2 Read the text. Does it mention any of the features you thought of?

James Bond's watches have a lot of useful features. First of all, they have a button that turns on a very bright blue light. This is useful for seeing in the dark. Secondly, they have a laser beam. This enables you to cut holes in walls to get away from people you don't like. The third feature is useful if you want to blow up a building. It's a detonator, so it enables you to leave before you set off an explosion. But the best feature is the hook. It's attached to a very thin strong wire and it's for lifting you up off the floor. First you fire the hook at the ceiling. Then you press another button and the wire pulls you up. James Bond's watches always have one other feature too. You can use them to tell the time.

3 Work with a partner. Ask and answer these questions.

1 What does the blue light enable you to do?
2 What can the laser beam do?
3 When is the third feature useful?
4 Which is the best feature and how does it work?
5 What do all James Bond's watches enable you to do?

4 Here are some more of James Bond's gadgets. Work with a partner and discuss these questions.

1 What are they?
2 What do they enable James to do?

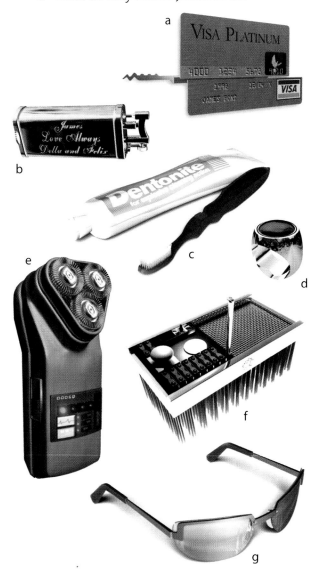

5 Match the gadgets to the descriptions.

1 This ring contains a tiny camera. It enables James to take photographs without anybody knowing.

2 This credit card is useful when it's time to pay the bill. But it's also for opening locked doors. It has a lock pick hidden inside.

3 These look like sunglasses, but really they are X-ray glasses. They enable James to see through people's clothes. They are useful when he wants to see if people have guns in their pockets.

4 You shouldn't clean your teeth with this toothpaste. It's a tube of plastic explosive and it enables James to create explosions.

5 This electronic razor is also a bug detector and it's very useful when James doesn't want people listening to his conversations. It enables him to find listening devices in his hotel rooms.

6 This isn't a normal hairbrush. It's a transmitter. It enables James to send messages in Morse code.

7 This lighter is really just a lighter. Some friends gave it to James as a present for being the best man at their wedding.

---

can, for, and enable

This is more than just a ring. You **can** take photographs with it. (It's possible.)
It's **for** taking photographs. (This is the purpose.)
It **enables** James to take photos without anybody knowing. (It makes it possible.)

---

6 Suggest endings for these sentences.

1 The lock pick enables …
2 These are special glasses. You can …
3 The plastic explosive is for …
4 This isn't a normal razor. You can …
5 The hairbrush is for …
6 The lighter enables …

7 Work with a partner. Look at the pictures in **4** again. Ask and answer questions.

A *What's this device for?*
B *It's for …-ing*

A *What can you do with this device?*
B *It enables you to …*

8 Here's another secret agent's kit. Match the words in the list to the items in the case.

1	belt	6	shirt button
2	binoculars	7	torch
3	chocolate bar	8	umbrella
4	comb	9	vacuum flask
5	pen	10	toothbrush

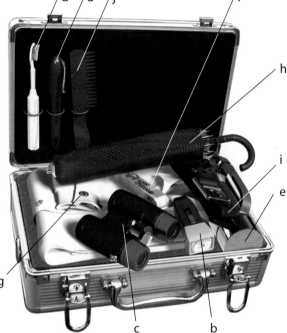

9 Work with a partner.

A – look at the information below.
B – look at file 14 on page 105.

A
You are a secret agent. Here are some things you need to do. Ask your partner about the items in the bag above. Find out which ones can help you. You need to:

1 climb down a 40 m high wall
2 make a guard fall asleep
3 open a locked door
4 check a room for listening devices
5 make a telephone call
6 photograph some documents
7 cut a hole in the wall and escape
8 blow up the building
9 see if a beautiful woman / handsome man has a gun in her / his pocket
10 offer her / him a drink.

Cause and effect

1 (4.1) What's this device for and how does it work? Label the parts with words from the list. Then listen and check your answers.

sharpener	blades	wood	gear
pencil holder	pivot	bucket	

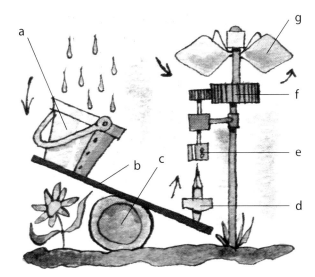

2 (4.1) Listen again and complete the sentences.

1 How do you .... it work?
2 You .... a pencil in the holder.
3 .... it rains, the bucket .... with water.
4 The wood is a ...., so .... you .... down on one end, the other end ....
5 A pencil sharpener. When the pencil rises, it .... inside.
6 And the wind .... the .... at the top ....?
7 They .... the gear and it .... the sharpener spin round.

Saying how things work

We can use *if* and *when* to say how one action causes another.
***When** it rains, the bucket fills up with water.*
***If** you press down on one end, the other end rises.*
Make can mean cause, or force something to happen.
*The wind **makes** the blades rotate. How do you **make** this work?*

3 Look at some more devices and match each one to the correct instruction.

1 Pull down on the ring.
2 Rotate the cam clockwise.
3 Increase the weight of the load on the left.
4 Turn the cog on the right anti-clockwise*.
5 Move the rod back and forth.
6 Open the lid.
7 Cut the string.
8 Connect the wires to the battery.

anti-clockwise **BrE** – counter-clockwise **AmE**

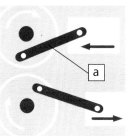

A crank

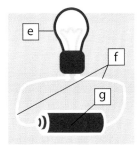

A pulley

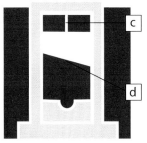

A guillotine

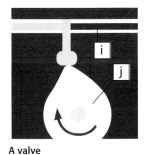

An electric circuit

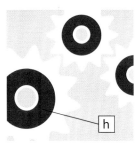

A gear

A valve

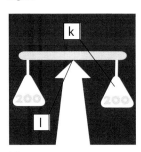

A lever

A boxing glove toy

4 Find these components in the pictures in **3**.

ring	cam	cog	rod	lid
string	battery	spring	pivot	pipe
bulb	blade	load	wires	

5 What happens when you follow the instructions in **3**?

Example
When you pull down on the ring, the load rises.

Which instructions can you reverse, and what happens if you do?

Example
If you let go of the ring, the load falls.

6 Work with a partner. Take turns asking and explaining how the devices work.

Example
A *How do you make the wheel turn round?*
B *You have to move the rod back and forth.*

7 Work in small teams. Design a machine to do one of these things.

1 Squeeze some toothpaste on to a toothbrush
2 Stick a stamp on an envelope
3 Screw a light bulb into its socket
4 Turn off an alarm clock
5 Crush and recycle an empty drink can

Try to include as many devices from **3** as you can. Draw a diagram of the machine and prepare to explain how it works.

8 Take turns showing your machines to the class. Which team's machine:

1 has the most components?
2 works best?
3 is the most unusual?

Checking and controlling

1 Look at the words *check* and *control* below. What words would you use in these situations in your language?

1 This switch **controls** the light. (*Turns it on and off*)

2 The thermostat **controls** the temperature. (*Stops it getting too hot or cold*)

3 The security guard will **check** your ID. (*Inspect it*)

4 Can you **check** the air in my tyres? (*Make sure they are OK*)

2 Complete the rule with *check* or *control*.

---

check and **control**

Use .... to talk about managing something, so it works correctly.
Use .... to talk about looking at something carefully to make sure it's correct, safe, or in good condition, etc.

---

3 Complete these sentences with *check* or *control*.

1 These knobs .... the volume.
2 .... the door's locked before you leave.
3 Can you .... the list to make sure we've got everything?
4 We can send people to the moon, and spaceships to Mars, but we still can't .... the weather.
5 They'll .... your passport at immigration control.
6 It's difficult to .... the vehicle when it's going round bends at high speeds.
7 You should .... the pressure of your tyres before you go on a long trip.
8 We .... the whole process from this room. We can shut everything down in seconds if we have to.

5 What happened?

Explaining what happened

1 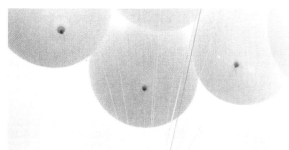 What do you think is happening in these pictures? Listen and read the story and find out.

This is a true story. On July 2 1982, Larry Walters, a 33-year-old North Hollywood truck driver, filled 45 weather balloons with helium and tied them to an aluminum* garden chair. Then he put on a parachute and climbed into the chair with lots of supplies, including some water, a pellet gun, a CB* radio, an altimeter, and a camera. He planned to fly across the desert.

aluminium **BrE** – aluminum **AmE**

CB radio: Citizen's band is a radio frequency for private radio communications.

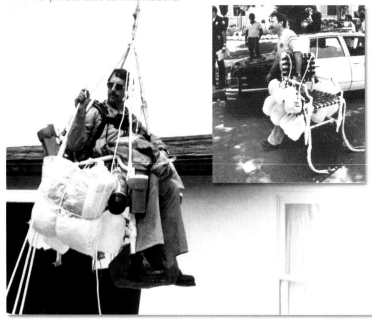

The chair was attached to the bumper of a friend's car with two ropes. But when his friends cut one of the ropes, the other rope snapped too. Larry shot up into the sky at more than 300 metres per second. It was so fast that his glasses fell off. He climbed quickly to about five kilometres above the ground.

Larry spoke to his friends on his radio. 'I'm floating across Los Angeles Harbour', he said. He wanted to fly to the Rocky Mountains, but the wind took him towards Long Beach Municipal Airport. Two pilots saw Larry and radioed air traffic control. They were all very surprised.

The air was thin three miles above the ground and Larry felt cold and dizzy. He shot some of the balloons with his gun, the chair floated down, and he landed safely.

Back on earth, Larry was famous. He appeared on lots of television shows and people loved him. But the Federal Aviation Administration didn't think it was funny and they wanted to take away his pilot's licence. They couldn't, because he didn't have one.

2 Ask and answer these questions with a partner.

1 Who was Larry Walters?
2 What was in the balloons?
3 What did he take with him on his flight?
4 What went wrong at take-off?
5 How high did he go?
6 How did he communicate with his friends on earth?
7 Did he plan to fly over the airport?
8 How did he come back to earth?
9 Why couldn't the Federal Aviation Administration take away his pilot's licence?

3 Underline all the verbs (actions) in the story. Find verbs that mean:

1 to break suddenly, often with a sharp noise
2 to travel slowly through the air.

Which verbs in the story are regular and which are irregular?

Regular and irregular verbs

Regular verbs end in *-ed* in the Past Simple. It's a short sound.
filled   tied   snapped   climbed

When the verbs end with a /d/ or /t/ sound, it's a long sound.
landed   wanted   floated

Many common verbs are irregular in the Past Simple:
fall → fell   take → took   cut → cut

4 The verb *be* is the most common verb in English. Its Present Simple forms are *am*, *is*, and *are*. What are its Past Simple forms? What are the other most common verbs in English? Can you guess?

5 You can find the twenty most common verbs in this puzzle. Read across →, down ↓, and diagonally up ↗ or down ↘.

G	C	U	H	B	S	A	Y
D	O	S	A	X	E	X	X
X	M	E	V	T	E	L	L
G	E	T	E	A	X	W	K
X	F	H	X	K	N	O	W
X	G	I	V	E	O	R	A
X	X	N	N	L	X	K	N
M	A	K	E	D	P	U	T

Many of these verbs have irregular forms in the Past Simple. What are they?

You can check your answers in file 2 on page 102, and there's a list of irregular verbs on page 118.

6 Think of an interesting holiday you went on, or an exciting trip you made. Take a few minutes to prepare, then tell some other students about it.

1 Where did you go?
2 Who were you with?
3 How did you travel?
4 What did you take with you?
5 Did everything go to plan?
6 What happened when you got back?

Rises and falls

1 How does your company measure quality? What statistics does it collect?

2 Read about some quality improvements at some other companies and answer the questions.

1 What kind of company is Color Graphics?
2 Why did the manager stop the presses?
3 What kind of changes did they make to the production processes?
4 What reduction did the company achieve?

A manager at Color Graphics stopped one of the company's printing presses one day and asked for everyone's attention. He showed the employees sixteen drums of waste ink and asked, 'How long does it take us to produce this waste?' Everyone was surprised to learn that they filled the drums in just one month. They began looking for ways to reduce the volume of waste. They made a lot of changes – just simple low-cost production changes, but they had a big effect. Over five years the company's total liquid waste fell from 1,525 barrels to 991 – a 35 per cent reduction.

Walton Electronics, a electronics manufacturer, upgraded the lighting in their workshops and ran an experiment at the same time. In one area, they installed brighter, high-intensity lights, but they left the original lighting in place. After a six-month trial period, they turned on the old lights again. The employees hated it! 'Turn the lights back on!' they shouted. The installation of the new lights cost $98,000 but Walton Electronics's energy bills went down by $48,000 in the first year. And that wasn't all. With the new lights, people could see better, so the quality of their work increased too – that was worth another $25,000 a year.

5 What improvement did Walton Electronics make to its workshops?
6 What experiment did they run?
7 How much did they save on electricity?
8 What was the value of the increase in quality?

3 We use lots of different verbs to talk about rises and falls. Look at the words in **bold** in these sentences. Can you think of other verbs you could use?

*At Walton Electronics, energy bills **went down** and the quality of the work **increased**. Color Graphics **reduced** its ink waste.*

Do these verbs describe upward ↑ or downward ↓ movements?

decrease	reduce	go up	rise	fall
improve	lower	drop	cut	

Which verbs have noun forms too?

Example
reduce → a reduction in waste

4 Look at some more statistics. Which ones refer to:

1 spending on raw materials?
2 pieces made per man-hour?
3 how much oil, gas, and electricity you use?
4 employees not coming to work?
5 materials you throw away?
6 materials you keep and use again?
7 goods and materials you have in stock?
8 the release of gas or radiation into the atmosphere?
9 time when you produce nothing?
10 the money you make when you sell something?
11 the money you pay to the government?
12 mistakes, errors?
13 staffing costs?
14 employees getting injured or things getting damaged?

Waste	– 1%	Material costs	– 4%
Defects	+ 2%	Recycled materials	– 15%
Taxes	– 2%	Emissions	– 6%
Profit	– 7%	Productivity	+ 7%
Downtime	+ 18%	Energy consumption	+ 10%
Accidents	– 6%	Absenteeism	– 5%
Inventory	+ 9%	Wages and salaries	+ 8%

5 Are the statistics in **4** good or bad? Which things do you try to increase, and which do you try to decrease?

6 What's the Past Simple of these verbs?

↗	↘
increase	decrease
rise	fall
go up	go down

Work with a partner. Discuss the statistics in **4**. Use the verbs.

A *Waste fell by 1 per cent this month.*
B *Yes, but defects rose by 2 per cent.*
A *Taxes decreased by …*

7 Work with a partner.

A – look at the information below.
B – look at file 16 on page 106.

A

1 This graph shows your company's operating costs over the last twelve months. Describe it to your partner so they can draw it. Explain the rises and falls.

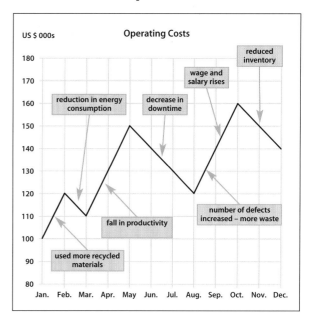

2 Listen to your partner's description of their company's CO₂ emissions over the last twelve months. Complete the graph below.

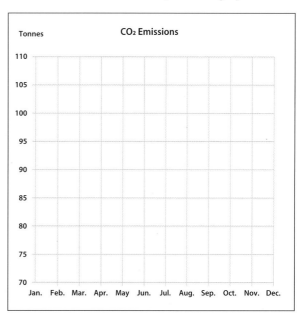

6 Can you fix it?

Troubleshooting

1 (6.1) Listen to some people talking about things that don't work. What kind of device or equipment is each conversation about?

2 (6.1) Listen to conversation 1 again and complete these questions.

1 .... the paper tray ....?
2 .... the connections?
3 .... plugged in?

What other things has he checked?

3 Work with a partner. Have a similar conversation about this vacuum cleaner. Use these words to help you.

A
It's not working!

B
dust bag full?
connections?
plugged in?
hose blocked?
fuse?
manual?
switched on?

4 (6.1) Listen to conversation 2 again. Complete these questions.

1 What happens when you ....?
2 Have you tried ....?
3 How soon ....?

5 Read the whole of conversation 2 with a partner.

A out of the heating vent.

B What happens when you ?

A . I've tried but it makes no difference.

B Have you tried ?

A Where's that?

B OK. I'll come and have a at it.

A  can you get here?

B Tomorrow.

A But here!

6 Work with some other students. Take turns explaining the problems below. The other students should suggest solutions, beginning *Have you tried ...?*

1 My computer's running slowly.
2 I can never remember my computer passwords.
3 I receive too much spam.
4 I want to lose weight.
5 I can't get to sleep at night.
6 I have hiccups.

Example
A *My computer's running slowly.*
B *Have you tried deleting files?*
A *Yes, but it didn't work.*
C *Have you tried ...-ing?*
B *Yes, but ...*

7 🎧 Listen to conversation 3 again.

1 What's missing?
2 Did he save it?
3 What are the possible causes of the problem?

Troubleshooting questions

Is it switched on / plugged in / blocked / full, etc.?
Have you checked the ...?
Have you tried ...-ing?
What happens when you ...?
How soon can you ...?

---

8 There are some problems with this refrigerator. Suggest possible causes.

Begin
It could be ... /
It might be ...

1 The interior light doesn't come on when you open the door.
2 The door makes a squeaking noise when you move it.
3 It's the wrong temperature. It's too cold.
4 There's a funny smell coming from inside.

9 Work in two teams.
Team A – you are computer experts.
Team B – you are car experts.

Team A

1 You have an old car and you're having a lot of problems with it. Make a list of the different problems.

Team B

1 You have an old computer and you're having a lot of problems with it. Make a list of the different problems.

2 Exchange your lists.

3 Read the problems **team B** is having with their computer. What could cause them? Prepare questions to ask about them.

3 Read the problems **team A** is having with their car. What could cause them? Prepare questions to ask about them.

4 Talk to the other team. Find out more about their problems and suggest solutions.

Repairs

1 Name the things in the pictures. Write the letters in the list. What can sometimes be wrong with these things?

Example
Bulbs can be burnt out, dirty, or broken.

1 bulb	......
2 screws	......
3 lock	......
4 rollers	......
5 tank	......
6 book	......
7 electrical connection	......
8 filter	......
9 battery	......
10 scissors	......
11 hose	......
12 paper tray	......

2 Find things in **1** that can be:

1 flat*
2 rusty
3 burnt out
4 stiff
5 blunt
6 torn
7 blocked
8 dirty
9 jammed
10 loose
11 empty
12 leaking

Think of other things that can be flat, rusty, burnt out, etc.

a flat battery – a battery goes flat **BrE**
a dead battery – a battery dies **AmE**

3 If a battery is flat, you have to replace it. If it's a rechargeable battery, you can recharge it. How can you fix problems with the other things?

4 (6.2) Listen to a conversation about three of the items in **1**. Which items are they and what are the problems?

5 (6.2) Complete the words. Then listen again and check your answers.

1 I'm r......... some safety tests.
2 The sound system i......... w..........
3 One of the speakers is m......... a f.........
   noise. We think it's a l......... connection.
4 Are the batteries f.........?
5 Perhaps the bulb's b......... o..........

Present Continuous

We use the Present Continuous to describe what's happening now.
I'm running some safety tests.
It's making a funny noise.

Change the word order to make questions and use *not* to make negatives.
What are you doing?
The sound system isn't working.

6 Your teacher will mime some repairs to the items in **1**. Watch and guess what they're doing. The verbs in the list will help you.

recharge	oil or lubricate	solder	tape
change	replace	clean	fill
sharpen	tighten	clear	unblock

Example

A *Are you recharging some batteries?*
B *No, I'm not.*
A *Are you soldering a wire?*
B *Yes, I am.*

7 Work with a partner. Take turns miming some verbs in **6**. Your partner must guess what you're doing.

8 Work with a partner.

A – look at the information below.
B – look at file 21 on page 108.

A

Describe this picture to your partner. Your partner has a similar picture, but there are eleven differences. Find and circle the differences. Why are the pictures different?

Present tenses

> ### Present Simple and Present Continuous
>
> Use the Present Simple for permanent or long-term situations and regular activities.
> *She works on the help desk, and she generally works the night shift.*
> Use the Present Continuous for temporary things that are happening now.
> *We're looking for the stairs. The lift isn't working today.*

1 Complete these sentences. Use the correct form of the verb in brackets.

1 I often .... (spend) two or three hours a day in meetings.
2 Can you have a look at the pump? It .... (make) a funny noise.
3 .... you .... (live) in Marseille?
4 Which hotel .... you .... (stay) in?
5 .... you .... (wait) for Mr Clark?
6 This wireless card .... (enable) me to connect to the web when I'm travelling.
7 How long .... it .... (take) you to get to work in the morning?
8 Our energy consumption usually .... (rise) in the winter.
9 A Can you hear me?
   B No, the microphone .... (not work).

2 Explain what you do on a regular basis:

1 What department division do you work in?
2 What jobs do you perform in a normal working day?

Explain what you're doing at the moment:

3 Are you working on any interesting projects? (What?)
4 Are you improving any systems or process? (What?)

Quick fixes

1 Read these conversations with a partner.

1 A What are you doing?
  B I'm folding this bit of paper up.
  A Yes, but why?
  B The table's wobbling. I'm going to put it under one of the legs.

2 A What are you doing?
  B I'm straightening this hanger.
  A I can see that, but why?
  B The television doesn't have an aerial. I'm going to connect this to one of the terminals.

3 A What are you doing?
  B I'm putting this battery in the oven.
  A I know, but why?
  B It's flat. I'm going to warm it up so it works a little longer.

2 Will the quick fixes work?

3 Suggest quick fixes for these problems:

1 a burnt out fuse
2 a broken fan belt
3 a screw hole that's too large for your screw
Work with a partner. Make similar conversations to the conversations in **1** about these problems.

Ups and downs

1 *Raise* and *rise* describe upward movement, but they mean different things. Complete the sentences.

raise and rise

When you pull down on the ring, it .... the load. (lifts it up)
The load .... (moves up)

2 Complete the sentences with *raises* or *rises*.

1 The sun .... in the east.
2 This switch .... the pressure.
3 The thermostat .... the temperature if it gets too cold.
4 Hot air ....
5 The cam wheel turns and it .... the rod.
6 The temperature .... in the summer.

3 Complete the rule. Write *by* or *to*.

by and to

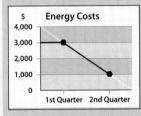

Energy bills fell by $2,000 in the 2nd quarter.   *Energy bills fell to $2,000 in the 2nd quarter.*

To describe a point something reaches, use ......
To describe the difference between two points, use ......

4 Complete the captions for some more graphs.

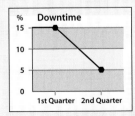

1 Downtime fell ...... 5%.   2 Hazardous waste increased ...... 3%.

Past Simple

1 Complete this story. Use the Past Simple of the verbs in the list.

be stay ~~want~~ decide have wake up	Four university students in Sydney, Australia *wanted* to go to a party. There ....¹ just one problem. The party was in Canberra on a Saturday night and they had a Chemistry examination the following Monday. The students ....² to go to the party and they all ....³ a great time. But on the Sunday morning they ....⁴ with headaches and ....⁵ in bed all day.
go ~~not get~~ think ask agree can't not have	The students *didn't get* back to Sydney until late on Monday – too late for the exam. So they went to speak to the Chemistry professor. "We ....⁶ to Canberra", they explained, "but on our way home we had a flat tyre. We ....⁷ a spare tyre in the car, so we ....⁸ change it. Can we take the examination tomorrow instead?" they ....⁹. The professor ....¹⁰ for a while, and then he ....¹¹.
be put see give turn over arrive	The four students studied all night and ....¹² for the exam the next morning. The professor ....¹³ them in four different rooms and ....¹⁴ them the questions. The first question carried five marks and it was very easy. The students ....¹⁵ very happy. Then they ....¹⁶ the page and ....¹⁷ the final question. It said "For 95 marks: which tyre?"

2 Do you know any jokes or funny stories? Think of one to tell the class.

7 I need some information

Questions

1 Read fast. You have just two minutes to answer these questions.

   1 Why is the network down on Tuesday afternoons?
   2 Who can't rent a room in the house in Hollingworth Street?
   3 What does TGIF stand for?
   4 Which notice is in the wrong section?

2 🎧 (7.1) Listen to three conversations and match them to the correct notices.

3 🎧 (7.1) Listen to conversation 1 again.

   1 What does the woman want?
   2 Why won't the man help?

4 Work with a partner. Practise asking questions with *What time ...?* Ask about:

   1 the mail room (open / close)
   2 Paul Peters (leave / arrive)
   3 the first aid course (start / finish)
   4 the first shuttle bus in the morning
   5 the help desk
   6 the TGIF party.

Example
A *What time does the mail room open?*
B *At eight thirty in the morning.*

5 🎧 (7.1) Listen to conversation 2 again.

   1 How long will it take to count the inventory?
   2 How long will the course last?

• COMPANY NOTICES

MAIL ROOM
Opening hours
Mon-Thurs
    8.30am—5pm
Fri   8am—4pm

Workplace
First Aid
Course
Level 2 Training Thursday
20th Nov
9.30–12.30
Contact Sharon Moss,
Safety Officer (ext 2453)

NETWORK SUPPORT
The Help Desk is open
Mon–Fri 8am–7pm.
Please note we perform regular
maintenance work on the network on
Tuesdays 17.00–19.00.
During this time there may be some
brief downtimes when users will be
unable to access the system.

Lynfield Plant
Shuttle Bus
Daily Schedule
All buses leave
from the main entrance

Dep	Arr
9.15	9.50
11.35	12.10
14.00	14.35
16.30	17.05

MOTORBIKE
FOR SALE
HARLEY DAVIDSON
2002 Blast
5000 miles. 3 years.
Single cylinder
Excellent condition
One careful owner. £3000
Contact Bill Peters 01962 4352792

• FOR SALE & WANTED

WANTED
A second hand piano
Can collect but must be under £250.
email: honeybun673892@yahoo.com

Moving to a smaller house. Must sell:
3 seater black sofa 21" colour
Cost £1200 new.   television
Will accept £600   £100

Judith Walters. Logistics, 6th floor.

LIFTS

MILTON KEYNES
Do you travel in from the Milton
Keynes area every day?
Looking for people to car pool.
I generally leave home at 7.15 and
get here for 8.30.

Paul Peters: 01908 6054723

take and last

We use *take* to say how much time we need to do something.
It takes me an hour to get to work.

We use *last* to say how long things continue.
One tank of petrol lasts me three days.

6 Complete these questions with *take* or *last*. Then ask and answer them with a partner.

1 How long does it .... to get to the Lynfield plant?
2 How long does *House of Frankenstein* ....?
3 How long do the TGIF parties ....?
4 How long does it .... Paul Peters to get to work?
5 How long do chess club meetings ....?
6 How long do the network downtimes ....?

7 (7.1) Listen to conversation 3 again. What's the apartment like?

What and How questions

We often use *what* and *how* with other words.
What size / colour / make / kind of ...?
How far / many / much / long / often ...?
What's it like? is a very general question. It means 'Tell me about it'.

What's your house or apartment like? Tell the class.

8 Complete these questions with *what* or *how*. Then ask and answer them with a partner.

1 .... make is Bill Peter's motorbike and .... old is it?
2 .... kind of piano does Honeybun want?
3 .... much does it cost to rent the apartment in Alicante in August?
4 .... colour is Judith's sofa and .... size is her television?
5 .... often do they hold TGIF parties?
6 .... much does Lisa weigh?
7 .... is the Riverside flat like?
8 .... many people can fit into the Alicante apartment?

9 Think of some things you want to advertise and write some notices. Read each other's notices and ask questions.

CLUBS & EVENTS

THANK GOODNESS IT'S FRIDAY
come and celebrate the end of the working week
TGIF party Every Friday, 5.30pm — late!
Duke of York pub across the road.
see you there!

This week Friday Nov 21st, 6pm
HOUSE OF FRANKENSTEIN
Starring Boris Karloff, 1945, 71 mins.
Tickets £8 in advance, £10 at the door.
Next Friday: The Matrix

Hi, I'm Lisa.
I weigh 3.9 kgs and I was born at 3.30am, Nov 12th.
Mummy and Daddy (Louise and Peter) thank everyone for the lovely flowers.

Chess Club meetings
Fridays: 8–10pm
in *George and Dragon*, Lynfield Road
Beginners welcome

ACCOMMODATION

Holiday apartment to let in ALICANTE
Sleeps 2 people (or 4 with the sofa bed in the lounge). 10-minute walk to the beach. 15-minute drive to the town centre.
May and September: £275 per week
June - August: £285 per week
October - April: £205 per week
Call Mark Thomas on 0737 7265394

Room available for rent in three bedroom house for female non-smoker.
Hollingworth Street - five minutes walk from the office
No dogs allowed.
Rent: **£350 per month** (does not include gas, electricity, water, etc.)

Riverside flat Fabulous ground floor flat in the Riverside area.
Beautiful tree-lined street. Very quiet.
Fireplace, hardwood floors, small back garden.
£800 per month.
Call John Simmonds on 01934 3425833, john_simm3@hotmail.com

Numbers

1 What dam is this and where is it? When was it built and how long did it take to build?

The Hoover dam is located 50 kms south-east of Las Vegas in the USA. It was built in the 1930s to stop flooding and provide irrigation, domestic water, and power. First they had to reroute the Colorado River through tunnels, and then they had to build the dam itself. It's 221 metres tall, 201 metres wide at its base, and it weighs nearly six billion tonnes. When it was finished, it was the largest dam in the world. Amazingly, the whole construction project was completed in just under five years.

2 🎧 7.2 Listen to some tourists at the dam. What questions do they ask their guide?

3 🎧 7.2 Listen again and underline the numbers you hear.

1	a 4 m kwh	b 4 b kwh
2	a 35,369,000m³	b 35,396,000m³
3	a 20.5 bar	b 21.5 bar
4	a 2,250,000 m³	b 2,500,000 m³
5	a 5,218	b 5,280
6	a 1934	b 1943
7	a 40 °C	b 44 °C
8	a $500,000	b $1,000,000
9	a $1	b $1.25

What do the numbers refer to?

4 Find the numbers in **3** that refer to these things and say them aloud.

1 The amount of concrete they used
2 The average amount of electricity generated by the dam in a year
3 The capacity of Lake Mead
4 The hourly pay of a crane operator
5 The average monthly payroll
6 The year most people worked on the dam
7 The maximum number of people working on the dam
8 The temperature the desert can reach
9 The water pressure at the bottom

Numbers

Large numbers
$1,000,000$ (or 1 m) = a million
$1,000,000,000$ (or 1 b) = a billion (a thousand million)
$1,000,000,000,000$ = a trillion (a million million)

Fractions
Notice how we say these fractions:
$1/4$ *a quarter* $1/3$ *a third* $1/2$ *a half*
$3/4$ *three quarters* $9/10$ *nine tenths*
We sometimes use fractions when we say large numbers.
$2,500,000$ *Two and a half million*

Years
Say years before 2000 in two parts. After 2000, say the number.
1934   *Nineteen thirty four*
2001   *Two thousand and one*

Money
We write the currency before the number, but we say it after the number.
$500,000   *Five hundred thousand dollars* NOT ~~dollars five hundred thousand~~
We say smaller units of currency after the number.
$1.25   *One dollar twenty five cents*

5 Write these numbers.

Example *Two million*   ....2,000,000......

1 Three trillion   ....
2 Two thirds   ....
3 Seven eighths   ....
4 Thirty five and a half   ....
   thousand
5 Half a billion   ....
6 Two and a quarter million   ....
7 Nineteen sixty six   ....
8 Two thousand and twelve   ....
9 Five hundred dollars   ....
10 Six euros and nine cents   ....

---

s or no s

Don't add s to words like *hundred*, *thousand*, *million*, etc. after a number.
Six *billion* tonnes (not ~~six billions tonnes~~ and not ~~six billions of tonnes~~)

We use s and *of* in expressions with no number.
Hundreds of men died.
They used billions of tonnes of concrete.

---

6 Complete these sentences. Form the correct expression with the number in brackets.

Three and a half <u>thousand</u> *people worked on the dam each day.* (thousand)
<u>*Thousands of*</u> *people worked on the dam each day.* (thousand)

1 At its base, the dam is two .... metres wide. (thousand)
2 They spent .... dollars constructing the dam. (million)
3 .... people worked on the dam. (thousand)
4 The average monthly payroll was five hundred .... dollars. (thousand)
5 The dam can generate over ten .... kilowatt-hours a year. (billion)
6 Lake Mead holds more than thirty five .... cubic metres of water. (million)
7 .... people died building the dam. (hundred)
8 Every year, ... tourists visit the dam. (thousand)

7 Work with a partner.

A – look at the information below.
B – look at file 15 on page 106.

A
1 Read this information to your partner so they can make a note of the numbers.

The Colorado River is 2,253 km long. When they were building the Hoover dam, they rerouted the river through tunnels. The tunnels had a total length of 4,860 m and they were over 15 m in diameter. They were lined with 229,359 m³ of concrete. The tunnels could carry over 5,500 m³ of water per second.

2 Your partner will read some more information about the dam. Make a note of the missing numbers.

They started laying the concrete in June ....[1] and finished in May ....[2]. The dam was built in blocks that varied in size from about ....[3] m² at the bottom to about .... m² at the top. To set the concrete, they laid more than ....[4] km steel pipe in the concrete and pumped icy water through it. The water came from a refrigeration plant that could produce ....[5] tonnes of ice a day.

8 Divide into two teams and hold a quiz.

Team A – look at file 22 on page 109.
Team B – look at file 31 on page 113.

8 What should we do?

Explaining rules

1 Do you have a GPS? (Would you like one?) What do people use them for?

2 Some people use their GPS to play a new game called *geo-caching*. Someone leaves a container and a message in a public place and other people have to find them. Read the message on the right and find out how to play the game.

Please Read

Congratulations! You've found my geo-cache!

I left this container here and posted its location co-ordinates on the Internet for other people to find. But if you found it by accident, you can play too. You just **have to** follow these instructions.

1 You **must** write your name and the time and date you were here in the logbook. This is very important.

2 There's a disposable camera in this container. You **don't have to** take a photo of yourself with it, but if you do, I'll post it on our website.

3 You **mustn't** take the logbook or disposable camera away.

4 There are some small toys and other items in this container. If you want something, you can have it. There's just one condition. You **have to** leave something in its place. You **don't need to** leave anything expensive and you **mustn't** leave anything dangerous, but you **must** leave something.

5 One last thing. You **need to** put this container back where you found it – so it's ready for the next person to find.

To learn more about geo-caching, visit our website at: http://www...

3 Do you understand the rules?

1 What information do you need to write in the logbook?

2 Must you take a photograph with the camera?

3 What will happen to your photograph?

4 Can you take anything you want from the container?

5 Can you take the container home with you?

4 Look at the phrases in **bold** in the message.

1 Find three phrases that mean something is necessary or obligatory.

2 Find their negative forms.

3 Do they all mean the same thing? What do they all mean?

5 Complete the rule. Write *don't have to*, *mustn't*, and *don't need to* in the correct spaces.

---

must, have to, and need to

In their positive form, *must*, *have to*, and *need to* have a similar meaning. We use them to say something is necessary or obligatory. But in their negative form, the meanings are very different.

To say something is wrong or prohibited, we use ....

To say something is not necessary, we use .... or ....

---

6 Complete the sentences with *don't have to* or *mustn't*.

1 It's easy to make a geo-cache and you .... spend a lot of money.

2 You .... leave your geo-cache in a dangerous place.

3 You .... put things like knives, drugs, alcohol, or fireworks in the container.

4 If you find a cache, you .... leave a message on the website, but it's nice if you do.

5 You .... break these three rules: take something, leave something, and write in the logbook.

6 Some people write jokes and stories in the logbooks. It's nice, but you ....

7 Leave the cache where you find it. You .... move a cache to a new location.

8 You .... leave food in geo-caches, because animals will smell it and destroy the container.

9 You .... be very rich to buy a GPS. They start at about $100.

10 You .... speak English to play geo-caching. It's played all over the world.

7 (8.1) Listen to the rules of another game. What game is it? Tell your teacher to stop the recording as soon as you think you know.

8 Work with a partner. Think of a game and prepare to describe the rules to the class. One person writes the rules and the other dictates and checks spelling, grammar, etc. You can choose any game you like, for example, monopoly, hockey, a card game.

9 Take turns to describe your rules, but don't say what the game is. The class must guess.

Making things work

1 (8.2) Listen to a conversation about one of these machines. Which machine is it about?

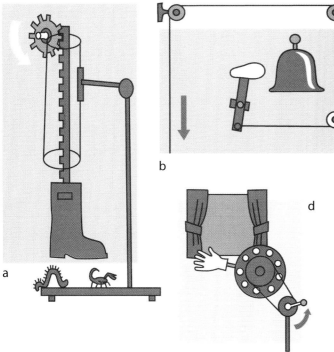

a

b

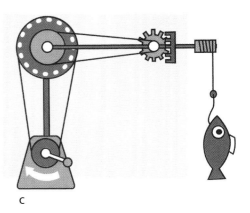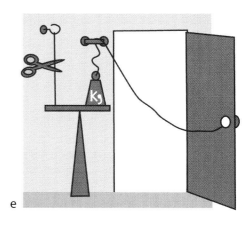

c

d

e

f

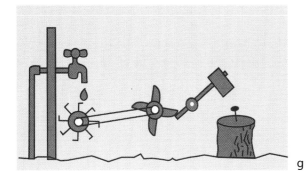

g

2 (8.2) They need to change the machine a little. Listen again and draw the changes on the picture.

3 Try to remember the missing words and complete the conversation.

A What do you t........?
B I'm not sure. How d........ it work?
A When someone c........ to the door, they p........ this string.
B So this is a p........?
A Yes, and these are p.........
B But is there a problem here? Does the hammer move c........?
A Oh, you're right. It r........ the wrong way.
B The bell n........ m........ over to the other side.
A The direction of the hammer h........ is wrong too. It needs r.........
B Do we need to put something u........ it, to stop it f........ too far?
A Yes, and perhaps it n........ a s........ to pull it back.

4 (8.2) Listen again and check your answers. Then read the conversation with a partner.

> ### needs doing
>
> We use *need + -ing* to talk about things that require work.
> It needs to be moved = It *needs moving.*
> It needs to be reversed = It *needs reversing.*

5 Complete these sentences. Use the correct form of the verbs in the list.

strengthen	sharpen	~~lower~~
reposition	lengthen	widen
enlarge	reverse	raise
speed up	tighten	

Example

The blade's too high. It needs <u>lowering</u>.

1 The string's too short. It needs ....
2 The pulleys are too low. They need ....
3 The handle's in the wrong place. It needs ....
4 The gears turn the wrong way. They need ....
5 The support's too weak. It needs ....
6 The street's too narrow. It needs ....
7 The hole's too small. It needs ....
8 The belts are too loose. They need ....
9 The blades are too blunt. They need ....
10 It's running too slow. It needs ....

6 Work in groups. Look at the machines in **1**. Answer these questions for each one.

1 What's it for?
2 What parts and components does it have?
3 What happens when you perform the action indicated by the arrow?
4 Does it work? (If not, what needs doing to make it work?)

7 Compare your solutions with the class. Do you all agree?

Damage

1 Look at the pictures and find things that are:

1 worn	5 bent	9 dusty
2 scratched	6 dented	10 corroded
3 chipped	7 crushed	
4 cracked	8 frayed	

2 Think of more things that can be worn, scratched, chipped, etc.

3 Work with the class.

1 Think of something you have that is broken or damaged. Write its name on a small piece of paper.

   My garage door opener

2 Take turns to describe the problem you're having. Say what needs doing.

   It doesn't always work. I think a part is bent or it could be corroded. It needs servicing.

3 Collect all the papers and put them in a bag. Shake it up and take turns pulling the papers out. Remember who owns the item, what's wrong with it, and what needs doing.

   Dieter has a problem with his garage door opener. He thinks a part is bent or corroded. It needs servicing.

9 *Take care*

Safety hazards

1 Where could you see a notice like this?
Do you have any similar safety precautions* where you work or study?

A precaution is something you do now to avoid hazards and danger, and to stop problems in the future.

> **Workshop safety precautions**
> **1** Wear goggles and ear protectors.
> **2** Do not leave things lying on the floor.
> **3** Wear short-sleeved shirts or roll up shirt sleeves.
> **4** Do not remove safety guards from machines.
> **5** Do not use electric tools when the work area is wet. Make sure plugs are earthed*.

earthed **BrE** – grounded **AmE**

2 Match these hazards to the correct precaution in **1**.

a Trips and falls   b Electric shocks   c Cuts   d Eye injuries and hearing damage   e Clothing getting caught up in machinery

3 (9.1) Listen to two conversations. Match each one to a hazard in **2**.

4 (9.1) Listen again and complete the sentences.

1 You .... roll up your sleeves.
2 You .... leave these boxes here.
3 Someone .... trip over them and hurt themselves.

Complete the rule. Write *should*, *shouldn't*, and *could* in the correct space.

> **should, shouldn't, and could**
>
> We use .... to talk about future possibilities.
> We use .... to say what's right or correct.
> We use .... to say what's wrong or dangerous.

5 Which hazards are these conversations about? Complete the sentences with *should*, *shouldn't*, or *could*. Then read them with a partner.

1 A The floor's wet.
   B Did someone spill some water?
   A Someone .... slip. We .... clean it up right away.
   B Yes, and we .... turn off all the machines. Someone .... get a shock.

2 A You .... use this machine without goggles. You .... injure your eyes.
   B I don't know where they are.

3 A Who took the guard off this machine? Someone .... have a nasty accident.
   B It takes longer to clean if it's on.
   A But you .... remove it. You .... cut yourself, or even lose a finger.

6 Find these things in the picture and write the letters in the boxes.

ladder	☐	goggles	☐
drawer	☐	hand cart	☐
sink	☐	glass flask	☐
drill	☐	fork-lift truck	☐
shelf	☐	crumbs	☐
lead*	☐	socket	☐

lead **BrE** – power cord **AmE**

7 Circle the safety hazards. How many can you find? Discuss them with another student.

A *The drill is on the floor.*
B *Yes, someone could trip over it.*
A *And the drill lead is worn.*
B *Yes, someone could get an electric shock.*

8 Explain what these people should and shouldn't do.

They shouldn't leave things lying on the floor. They should make sure electrical equipment is in good condition.

9 Work in small groups. You are responsible for training some new apprentices on safety in your workplace.

1 Brainstorm different safety precautions people in your workplace should take. Write a list.
2 Prepare to explain your list to new apprentices. Explain what they should and shouldn't do, and what could happen if they don't take precautions.
3 Present your safety precautions to the class and answer any questions they have.

Instructions

1 How do you change the oil and oil filter in a car?
Look at the diagrams and explain what you have to do.

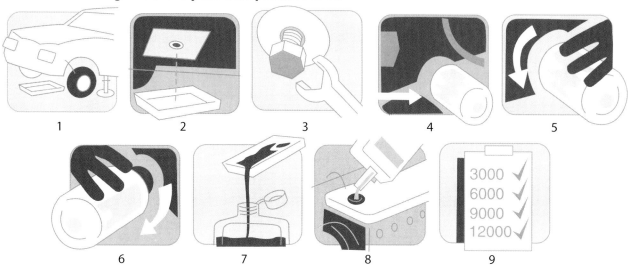

1   2   3   4   5

6   7   8   9

2 Here are the instructions, but they are muddled up. Match each instruction to the correct picture.

- [ ] Then locate the oil filter.
- [ ] Lower the car to the ground slowly and pour new oil into the engine. Check thoroughly under the car for any leaks and clean up any spilt oil.
- [1] Check the handbrake is on and jack up the front of the car. Place a shallow pan on the ground under the engine.
- [ ] Screw in the new filter, rotating clockwise this time. Don't screw it too tightly.
- [ ] Repeat this process regularly to keep your engine running well – every 5,000 kilometres is recommended.
- [ ] Unscrew the drain plug and wait for the oil to drain completely. It will flow out easily. Replace the plug and do it up tightly with a wrench.
- [ ] Remove the drain pan and carefully pour the old oil into a container you can seal for disposal.
- [ ] Make sure that it's directly underneath the engine's drain plug.
- [ ] Remove the filter by rotating it gently anti-clockwise. Pour any oil from the filter into the pan.

3 Work with a partner.

1 Where should you put the drain pan?
2 How do you remove the old oil from the engine?
3 How should you put the drain plug back on?
4 Should you screw in the new oil filter tightly?
5 What should you do with the old oil?
6 How often do you need to do this?

Adjectives and adverbs

Adjectives describe things:
a *shallow* pan, the *old* oil, the *new* filter

Adverbs describe actions – they answer the question 'How do you do it?'
Rotate it *gently*.
Check *thoroughly*.
Do it up *tightly*.

4 Complete these sentences with words from the list. Use each word once.

thorough/thoroughly	tight/tightly
careful/~~carefully~~	slow/slowly
easy/easily	

Example

It's icy outside, so please drive carefully.

1 I can't unscrew this nut. It's too ....
2 It's very .... to operate. A child could do it.
3 I don't want any mess, so make sure you clean up ....
4 Make sure you screw the lid on .... We don't want any gas to escape.
5 Be .... not to touch any of these parts. They're very delicate.
6 I don't have broadband. I'm using a 56k modem so it's very ....
7 I was well prepared for the test and answered all the questions ....
8 What caused the accident? We need a .... investigation.
9 You need to lose weight .... to stay healthy. Try to lose just half a kilogram a week.

Forming adverbs

You can make adverbs from most adjectives by adding -ly.

quick → quickly   gentle → gently

But some common adverbs are irregular.

Adjective	Adverb
good	*well*
hard	*hard*
fast	*fast*

5 Write down two things that you:

1 do badly
2 do well
3 do fast
4 work hard at.

Work with a partner. Read the things in your list in a different order. See if they can guess which adverb you are talking about.

6 What are these people doing? How can you do these tasks? Which things can you do: quickly, slowly, carefully, accurately, firmly, gently, evenly, tightly, thoroughly, regularly, safely, carelessly, poorly, etc?

What different tasks do you need to do in your work? How do you need to do them?

7 Play a game with the class. Each person needs two small pieces of paper.

1 On one piece of paper, write an action. On the other piece, write an adverb. Put all the actions in one pile and the adverbs in another. Keep the actions and adverbs separate.
2 Each student takes one action and one adverb from the piles. They have to act out the action in the manner of the adverb. The class must guess what the action and the adverb are.

Questions

1 Here are some questions a visiting colleague might ask. Complete them with *who, what, where,* or *how.*

<u>*Where*</u> *can I get a cup of coffee and something to eat?*

1 .... are the photocopiers?
2 .... do I need to do to log on to the network?
3 .... can give me a computer password?
4 .... do you keep your paper supplies?
5 .... does the phone system work?
6 .... can help me get a security pass?
7 .... happens if there's a fire?
8 .... long does it take to get to the city centre from here?
9 .... can I park my car?
10 .... time does the building close at night?
11 .... many lifts are there in this building?
12 .... systems do you have for recycling rubbish?

2 Work with a partner. Take turns asking and answering the questions.

3 Complete these questions with *take* or *last,* then ask and answer them with a partner.

1 How long do the batteries in your watch normally ....?
2 How long does it .... you to fall asleep at night?
3 How long does it .... for light rays from the sun to reach the earth?
4 How long does milk ...., if you keep it in the fridge?
5 How long do the bubbles in champagne ....?
6 How long does it .... to learn English?

Saying how

Adjectives and adverbs

We use adjectives to describe things and adverbs to describe how we do things.
*It's a **heavy** box. Lift it **carefully**.*
*The door is **closed**. Open it **gently**.*
We can also use adverbs to describe adjectives and past participles.
*The box is **really** heavy.*
*The door is **tightly** closed.*

Choose the correct word.

1 This bottle opener is *poor/poorly* designed.
2 I need an *immediate/immediately* decision.
3 His car was *bad/badly* damaged in a crash.
4 I'm afraid it wasn't packed *proper/properly*.
5 The handle isn't very *strong/strongly*.
6 Put the bread in a *warm/warmly* oven.
7 There's something *serious/seriously* wrong.
8 The wires are *wrong/wrongly* connected.
9 The hole's *terrible/terribly* small.

Avoiding problems

1 Have you ever:

1 left a bicycle outside in the rain?
2 forgotten to turn off your mobile phone*
   in the cinema*?
3 sent fragile goods in the mail?
4 touched a light switch with wet hands?
5 put coffee grounds down the sink?
6 failed to update your antivirus software?
7 left your torch* switched on when you're
   no longer using it?
8 had a cigarette in a room with a sensitive
   smoke detector?
9 stayed outside in the sun too long on a
   very hot day?

mobile phone **BrE** – cell phone **AmE**
cinema **BrE** – movie theater **AmE**
torch **BrE** – flash light **AmE**

2 Say what could happen if you do the things
in **1**.

Example
*If you leave a bicycle outside in the rain, it could
go rusty.*

3 Say how you can avoid these problems.

Example
You should always try to keep bicycles under cover.

Safety guidelines

1 How could a filing cabinet cause an accident?

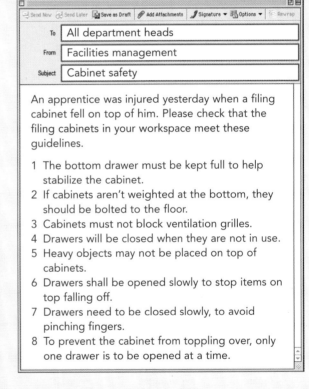

To	All department heads
From	Facilities management
Subject	Cabinet safety

An apprentice was injured yesterday when a filing
cabinet fell on top of him. Please check that the
filing cabinets in your workspace meet these
guidelines.

1 The bottom drawer must be kept full to help
   stabilize the cabinet.
2 If cabinets aren't weighted at the bottom, they
   should be bolted to the floor.
3 Cabinets must not block ventilation grilles.
4 Drawers will be closed when they are not in use.
5 Heavy objects may not be placed on top of
   cabinets.
6 Drawers shall be opened slowly to stop items on
   top falling off.
7 Drawers need to be closed slowly, to avoid
   pinching fingers.
8 To prevent the cabinet from toppling over, only
   one drawer is to be opened at a time.

2 Read the memo. Which guidelines describe:

a things you have to do?
b things you shouldn't do?

3 Explain what's wrong with the filing cabinet
in **1**.

Example
*The bottom drawer is probably empty so it's
unstable. It has to be filled.*

10 What's it like?

Shapes

1 What are these objects? Find a:

1	traffic cone	6	CD
2	clock	7	can
3	protractor	8	dice
4	stamp	9	ball bearing
5	floppy disk	10	traffic sign

What shape are they?

2 Find something:

1	circular	6	cylindrical
2	rectangular	7	triangular
3	square	8	oval
4	cubic	9	conical
5	semi-circular	10	spherical

3 Draw the correct shapes in the boxes.

a b c

d e f

g h

i j

circle

square   triangle   oval

rectangle   semi-circle   cube

cylinder   sphere   cone

4 Say these words aloud. Does the stress change?

1 triangle – triangular
2 circle – circular
3 rectangle – rectangular
4 cylinder – cylindrical
5 sphere – spherical

Example
triangle ●●●   *triangular*   ●●●● (the stress moves)
circle ●●   *circular* ●●● (no change)

5 Work with a partner. Ask and answer questions about the objects in **1**.

Example
A *What shape is the traffic cone?*
B *It's conical.*

Describing shape

We sometimes describe shape by saying what things look like.

It's a dome.

It's a pyramid.

We can also add *-shaped* to the word.

a heart-shaped box

a star-shaped cookie cutter

6 Work with a partner. Ask and answer questions about these structures.

Example
A *What shape is the building on the left?*
B *It's a dome. What shape is its doorway?*

7 You have three minutes to design your dream home. Draw a sketch of it. Try to include as many shapes as you can.

8 Put your sketch away and work with a partner.

A – you are an architect. Your partner is your client. Listen to their description of their dream home, draw it, and suggest improvements.

B – You are the client. Tell your partner what kind of home you want.

Classifying

1 What is this thing?

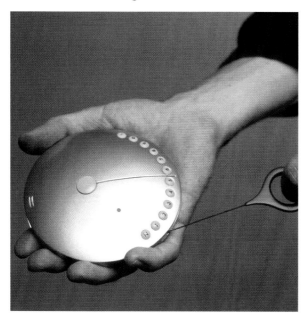

Read the three descriptions. Which one is correct?

1 This powerful instrument can locate metal objects that are up to three metres underground. When you pull the cord, it generates a magnetic field and picks up a signal from the target objects.

2 This device never needs charging from a mains supply*. It enables you to communicate with someone in another building, town, or country. Charge the generator by pulling the cord and you will have power for over five minutes of talking.

3 This electronic gadget is an executive toy. It moves up and down along the cord and you can program it to rotate at different speeds and heights. You can even program it to reverse direction.

mains supply **BrE** – AC supply **AmE**

Look at file 26 on page 111 to find out which description is correct.

Devices and equipment

Device is a very general term for a tool or piece of equipment, for example, *a labour-saving device, a security device*. But we have a lot of other words for equipment.

machine – equipment with moving parts that works with electricity or a motor

instrument – for doing delicate and precise work, where you need to be exact

appliance – a piece of electrical equipment we use in our house

2 Which description said it was:

1 a kind of yoyo?
2 a type of metal detector?
3 a sort of telephone?
4 an instrument?
5 a device?
6 a gadget?

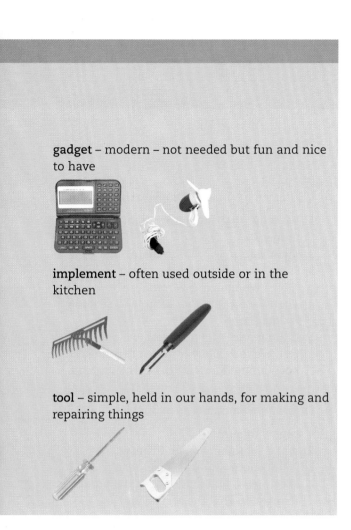

gadget – modern – not needed but fun and nice to have

implement – often used outside or in the kitchen

tool – simple, held in our hands, for making and repairing things

3 In what ways could you classify these things?

1 a washing machine
2 a hammer
3 a motorized cup that stirs your tea for you
4 a vacuum cleaner
5 a compass
6 a garden spade
7 a computer

Example
washing machine – It's a machine or an appliance.

4 Think of more examples of machines, appliances, instruments, etc.

5 🎧 (10.1) Listen to three descriptions. They are puzzles. What are the people describing? Tell your teacher to stop the recordings when you think you know.

6 🎧 (10.1) Listen to one of the descriptions again. Listen to each sentence one by one. Does it describe:

1 what the thing does or what it's for?
2 what the thing is like (its shape, colour, size, etc.)?
3 its parts?
4 the class of thing it is (building, tool, vehicle, etc.)?
5 something else? (What?)

7 Work with a partner. Think of an object and write a similar description. It can be a tool, a toy, a musical instrument – any object you like. You are going to read your description to the class and they must guess what it is, so don't make it too easy.

Then take turns reading your descriptions to the class. Which descriptions were the most difficult to guess?

8 Work with a partner to complete this crossword.

A – look at the crossword below.
B – look at file 24 on page 110.

A
There are no clues to this crossword. Your partner has the words you need and you have the words your partner needs. Make up clues to help your partner. You can't say the missing words, but you can describe them.

¹S				²R		³		
E				O		⁴O	V	A	⁵L
R	⁶	⁷H		L				
V		O		⁸L	A	S	E	R	
E		O		E				
R		K	⁹	R		¹⁰K		
						I		¹¹
¹²B			¹³P	¹⁴T		L		
A	¹⁵D	I	A		L		
N	R	P	X		¹⁶G	E	A	R
¹⁷K	I	E	I		R		
	L			¹⁸	A		
¹⁹	L				M		

Testing

1 What do these words mean?

Flammable	Inflammable
Non-flammable	Flame

2 (11.1) Listen to someone describing flammability tests on fabrics.

1 How many tests do they describe?
2 What does each test measure?
3 Which test is the most important?

3 (11.1) Listen again and complete the sentences.

1 We take .... and attach them to metal frames.
2 Then we .... to them.
3 First we see how fast the fabric .... We time it.
4 Then we test another sample to see how far the flames ....
5 If the fabric .... that test, we do a third test. We take a larger piece of fabric and see how far and how fast the flames spread.

4 Find words and phrases in **3** which mean:

1 begins to burn
2 make something begin to burn
3 is not successful, has a bad result
4 specimens, small quantities of a product that show what the rest is like
5 expand to cover a larger area.

5 Read this written description of the same tests. How is the language different?

Flammability test procedure

Fabric samples are attached to a metal frame and *a small flame is applied*. In the first test, the time the fabric takes *to ignite* is recorded. In the second test, *the distance* the flames spread is measured. If the fabric fails the second test, *a third test is performed*. A larger sample is taken and *timings over distance are calculated*.

Look at the words and expressions in *italics*. Find more informal ways to say these things in **3**.

Example
a small flame is applied = *we set fire to them*

Present passive

We form the passive with the verb *be* and the past participle.
Active: *We attach a piece of fabric to a metal frame.*
Passive: *A piece of fabric **is attached** to a metal frame.*
Active: *We take larger samples of the fabric.*
Passive: *Larger samples of the fabric **are taken.***

6 We often use passives in written procedures. Find examples of passives in the written description of the flammability test procedure in **5**.

7 These pictures show three different quality tests for ties. What is each test measuring? What's the procedure?

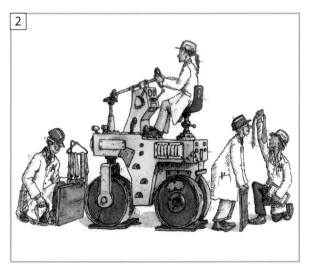

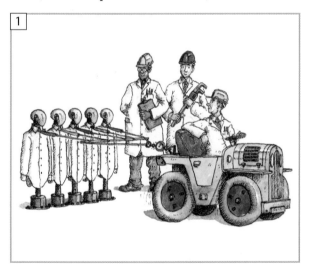

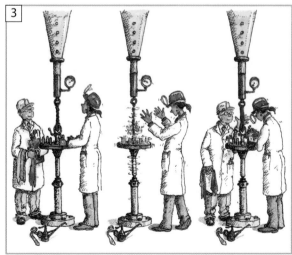

8 Complete this description of the tests. Put the verbs in brackets into the passive.

In the first test, the samples *are tied* (tie) around the necks of five dummies. The ends ....[1] (attach) to a metal bar on the back of a car, and the car ....[2] (drive) away. The distance the car can travel before the ties tear ....[3] (measure).

In the second test, some samples ....[4] (fold) and ....[5] (place) under pieces of wood and heavy pressure ....[6] (apply). Then they ....[7] (examine) for creases. If the ties pass this test, a second crease test ....[8] (perform).

A sample tie ....[9] (hang) from a ring and the ends ....[10] (fasten) to a wooden wheel. The wheel ....[11] (rotate) many times. When it cannot be rotated any more, it ....[12] (release) and the sample ....[13] (inspect).

9 Brainstorm some more quality tests for ties. What other things could you measure?

Work with some other students. Create another test for ties. Draw a picture or diagram and prepare to show it to the class.

10 Explain your test to the class. Explain what it measures and how it works. Then write a description of the test procedure. Use passives where necessary.

Understanding instructions

1 These inventions have all received US patents.

1 What are they for?
2 What parts and components do they have?
3 How do they work?

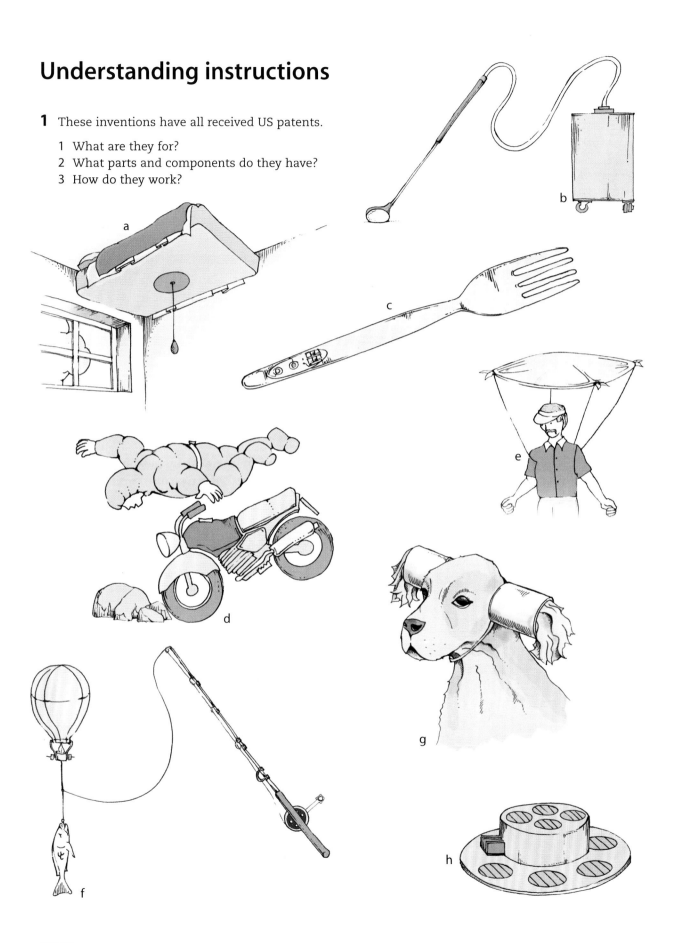

2 Find out if you were right. Match these descriptions to the devices.

1 Put on this suit before going for a ride. In a crash, it swells with compressed gas and protects your head, arms, body, and legs.

2 Pull the rope to lower this floating bed to the floor at bedtime. It is filled with helium gas, so you can store it on the ceiling when not in use.

3 Lose weight by eating with this fork. It has sensors that time your mouthfuls. When the red light comes on, you wait. When the green light comes on, you take another mouthful.

4 Attaching your golf club to the high pressure pump makes your balls go further. The golf club is hollow and the pump forces water through the hose, down into the club and out of the back.

5 Keep cool on hot days by wearing this sunhat. Its solar cells power a small radiator at the front.

6 Put these tubes on your dog before serving its dinner. They stop its ears falling in its food.

7 Use this device to lift fish out of the water. The balloon floats on the surface. When a fish bites, it fills with gas, hooks the fish, and lifts it out of the water. Then it's easy to bring in.

8 Wearing this balloon on hot days protects you from sunburn. It is filled with helium gas so it floats above your head.

Two-part instructions

Sometimes instructions contain extra information:
a *Do X by doing* Y
   = Y causes X
b *Do X before doing* Y
   = You have to do X first
c *Do X (in order) to do* Y or *Doing X does* Y
   = X causes Y

3 Look at the sentences in the texts in **2**. What two-part instructions do they contain?

Example
*Put on this suit before going for a ride =
instruction b*

4 Choose the correct answer to complete these sentences.

a Use this balloon to *protect/protecting* yourself from the sun.
b *Wear/wearing* this hat keeps you cool.
c Protect your body by *wear/wearing* this safety suit.
d Pull fish out of the water easily by *use/using* this device.
e Attach this pump to your golf club before *hit/hitting* the ball.
f Put these tubes on your dog's ears *keeping/to keep* them clean.
g *Use/using* this fork helps you lose weight.
h Lower the bed to the floor before *get/getting* in it.

5 Work in pairs or small groups. Think of three more inventions. They can be any inventions you like, for example: the mobile phone, the electric light bulb, the submarine.

Write some brief two-part instructions for the invention and explain how it works. One person should write and the others should dictate and check spelling, etc. Then read your instructions to the class. The class must guess what the invention is.

12 *Watch out!*

Warnings

1 Where could you see these signs and labels?

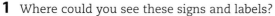

e — Please wait to be seated

f — Contraindications MAY CAUSE DROWSINESS. DO NOT OPERATE MACHINERY AFTER USE. not exceed the stated dose. Stop taking the medicine if you experience the following: unexpected wheezing, shortness of breath, rash, ...sing or facial swelling. Headaches, dizziness, vertigo, tinnitus ...ual disturbances, sensitivity to light and occassionally

g — Keep lid securely fastened. Do not drink or inhale. Avoid contact with skin.

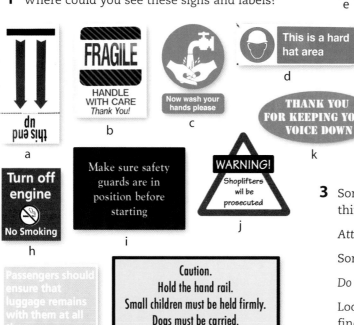

a — this end up

b — FRAGILE HANDLE WITH CARE Thank You!

c — Now wash your hands please

d — This is a hard hat area

k — THANK YOU FOR KEEPING YOUR VOICE DOWN

l — Space reserved for employee of the month

m — Important! Not intended for indoor use. Never direct at another person.

h — Turn off engine No Smoking

i — Make sure safety guards are in position before starting

j — WARNING! Shoplifters wil be prosecuted

n — Passengers should ensure that luggage remains with them at all times.

o — Caution. Hold the hand rail. Small children must be held firmly. Dogs must be carried.

2 Say which one you might see:

1. on a bottle of medicine
2. on a container of cleaning fluid
3. at a building site
4. in a store
5. in a restaurant
6. in a library
7. in a petrol station
8. in a car park
9. in a toilet or restroom
10. at an airport
11. on something that breaks easily
12. on a box or crate
13. on a piece of machinery
14. on an escalator
15. on a firework.

3 Some warnings contain instructions to do things.

Attention!   Please   Make sure

Some contain instructions NOT to do things.

Do not …   Never …   … must not be …

Look at the signs and labels in **1** again and find more words and expressions we often use in warnings. Do they contain positive or negative instructions?

4 Read this text about warning labels. Do you agree with the writer?

WARNING:
There are too many warnings

Have you seen packets of peanuts that say 'Warning: contains nuts'? Isn't it obvious that a packet of peanuts contains nuts? Of course companies need to protect themselves from expensive lawsuits, but are all these warnings helpful? A label on a bottle of children's cough medicine says 'Do not drive a car or operate machinery'. Do parents really need to know this? The problem is when there are too many warnings, people don't read them. And that's dangerous.

5 An organization in Michigan, USA holds a competition every year for the funniest warning labels. Here are some of the winners. Match the products to their warnings.

a birthday cake candles

b hairdryer

c iron

d snowblower

e underarm deodorant

f dishwasher

g wheelbarrow

h sleeping pills

i ink cartridge

j buggy*

buggy **BrE** – stroller **AmE**

1 Do not use on roofs.
2 Do not allow children to play inside.
3 Remove child before folding.
4 Warning: may cause drowsiness.
5 Caution: do not spray in eyes.
6 Do not eat toner.
7 Never use while sleeping.
8 Not intended for highway use.
9 Do not use soft wax as earplugs or insert into any other body cavity.
10 Never use on clothes while they are being worn.

You can read the answers in file 18 on page 107.

6 Work in groups. Write some warning labels for these products. They can be funny or serious. Try to use as many words and phrases from the list as you can.

Warning! Important! Attention! Caution! Danger!	... must be ... Not intended for ... May cause ...
	Thank you for (-ing) Please ...
Do not ... Never ... Avoid ... No (-ing)	Keep ... ... must not be ... ... should be ...
	Make sure ... (Do X) before (-ing)

7 Read your labels to the class. Which group has:

1 the most warnings?
2 the funniest warnings?
3 the most useful warnings?

Making suggestions

1 What kinds of security problems does your company have? What does it do to try to stop:

1 stealing?
2 spying?
3 people making private photocopies?
4 people making private telephone calls?
5 hackers breaking into your intranet?
6 misuse of the Internet by employees?
7 unauthorized people entering the company?

2 Look at these security devices. What are they? How could they be used? What security problems could they solve?

a

b

3 Listen to different people talking about the devices. Match each conversation to the correct picture.

c

d

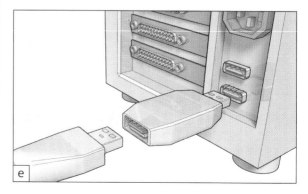

e

4 (12.1) Listen again and complete the sentences.

1 A What we need is a .... camera.
   B Yes, it has to be ....
   C Then .... install this?

2 A It's simple.
   B But very ....
   A .... install one in front of all the doors.

3 B It's amazing!
   C It's .... !
   A .... some for our trucks?

4 A Everybody's eyes are different. It's 100 per cent ....
   B Hmmm.
   A .... look into it.

5 B If someone .... working – like computer games, Internet chatrooms –
      ....
   C .... try it?

5 Find five expressions used to make suggestions in **4**.

1 Which one is followed by -ing?
2 Which one is the strongest suggestion?
3 What are the question and negative forms of I think we should ...?

6 Look at these reactions to ideas. Are they positive (+) or negative (–)?

1 It'll save time.
2 That'll work.
3 Yes, but ...
4 Exactly!
5 That's crazy!
6 That's a great idea.
7 It's too expensive.
8 It's interesting, but ...
9 Maybe, but don't forget ...
10 Yeah! Why not?

7 Work with some other students. Read the problems and make suggestions. Use the phrases in the box below. Don't forget to respond to each other's ideas.

Making suggestions

Why don't we ...?   How about ...(-ing)?
I think we should ...   Couldn't we ...?   We could ...

1 Someone has stolen a lot of expensive tools and equipment from your workshops in the last three months. It could be someone who works at your company or it could be the cleaning staff.
2 You want to avoid getting viruses in your computers.
3 You are worried about hackers breaking into your computer system and stealing company secrets.
4 One of your night-time security guards is very unreliable. He's often late and you think he sometimes falls asleep at work.
5 The police have warned you that a group of terrorists are planning to plant an explosive device in your factory / offices.
6 Someone in your department is spying for one of your competitors. You think you know who it is, but you are not 100 per cent sure.
7 One of your company's engineers went abroad to install a machine and he was kidnapped. You have received a note from his kidnappers demanding $10,000,000.

8 Work with some other students.

1 Design one or more security devices to protect these things:
   a your company's PCs
   b employees' mobile phones
   c employees' personal possessions (briefcases, wallets, handbags*, etc.)
   d company buildings
   e company vehicles.

handbag **BrE** – purse **AmE**

Draw a diagram of your device(s) and prepare to explain it to the class.

2 Look at each other's security devices and find out how they work. Try to suggest improvements.

Shapes

Compare the two figures.

1 How many triangles are there?
2 How many quadrilaterals are there?
3 Which shapes are the same size?
4 What is the area of the rectangle? What is the area of the square?
5 Is there something strange about this?

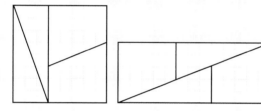

Test procedures

1 These photos all show different product tests. What do you think the tests are and how are they performed?

1

2

3

4

2 Complete these descriptions of the test procedures using the passive form of verbs in the boxes. Match each description to the correct picture.

place   insert   ~~prick~~   indicate   take

a The patient's finger is pricked with the yellow lancet to extract blood. A small drop of blood ....¹ on a test strip. Next, the strip ....² in the meter and a reading ....³. The quantity of glucose in the blood ....⁴ by a colour change.

compare   place   count   apply

b 80 mosquitoes ....⁵ in a glass cage. Different mosquito repellents ....⁶ to the arms of five volunteers. The volunteers then place their arms in the cage for five minutes. When they remove their arms, the bites ....⁷ and the results ....⁸.

attach   give   examine   record

c The subject ....⁹ drugs containing different amounts of alpha-linoleic acids. Wires ....¹⁰ from his / her head to an electroencephalograph (EEG). The subject then watches a television screen and his / her brain's electrical activity ....¹¹. The effects of the different drugs on his / her brain activity and memory ....¹².

position   use   note   pull

d Tests like these ....¹³ to assess the safety of children's toys under pressure. A toy ....¹⁴ between a vice and a suspended grip. The grip ....¹⁵ upwards with a force exceeding 50 kilograms until either the head or leg joints break off. The point at which it snaps ....¹⁶.

Manuals

1 Do you ever have to read equipment manuals that are written in English? (What are they for?)

2 Look at the first page of this manual.

CONTENTS	

Which chapter should you turn to for information on:

1 how to start the equipment, run it, and shut it down?
2 how to store it if it's idle?
3 how to take the equipment out of its boxes and cases?
4 how to throw it away when you no longer need it?
5 assembling and installing the equipment?
6 what the equipment can and can't do?
7 what to do if it goes wrong?
8 what to do if someone is hurt or there's a serious problem?
9 what you need to do to keep it functioning well?
10 who to contact if it breaks down in the first six months?

3 In which chapter of the manual could you find these pieces of information?

Disconnect and remove cylinders when not in use. Keep cylinders upright in a dry place at a temperature not exceeding 23°.

1

Start the engine by placing your foot on the top of the wheel, holding the handle bar, and pulling the rope starter.

2

All parts are guaranteed against defects in the workmanship or material for one year (12 months) from the date of delivery. Refer to page 84 for a list of dealers in your area.

3

To ensure smooth operation, lubricate all moving parts every 3–4 weeks.

4

Take special care when removing the valve from the bubble wrap and avoid touching the glass tubing.

5

Thank you for choosing Robinsen's. Please read the following procedures for positioning and connecting your new speakers and making the initial adjustments to the subwoofers.

6

In case of gas leaks, shut down the equipment immediately, disconnect from mains electricity supply, and vacate the building.

7

The projector automatically adjusts the 'brightness' level. However, it will not adjust the 'contrast' level. See page 63 for information on how to adjust the contrast manually.

8

Symptom	Possible cause	Action
Cannot connect	Main switch not on	Turn on main switch
	Battery failure	Recharge battery
	PC board failure	Replace PC board

9

Never attempt to pour old engine oil down the drain. Use an authorized hazardous waste management facility.

10

13 Out and about

Giving directions

1 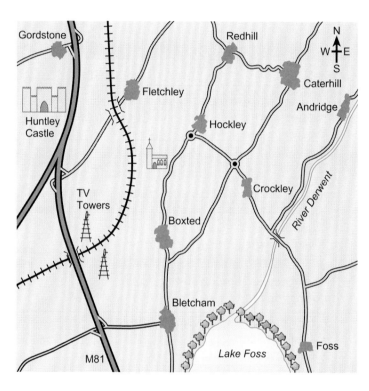 Listen to someone asking for directions. Draw the route they should take on the map.

2 Listen again and complete the sentences.

1 You need to get on the motorway and .... south.
2 .... going for five miles or so.
3 You'll go .... a castle on the right.
4 Take the left-hand .... and go over the railway lines. Then .... the motorway at the next exit.
5 Turn left at the .... in Bletcham.
6 Head .... Boxted. But don't go .... Boxted. Turn right just .... it. The road is .... to Caterhill.
7 Then you'll come to a roundabout*. Take the ....·
8 It .... a river – it's very pretty.
9 You'll see our factory .... the ....
10 You can't .... it!

roundabout **BrE** – traffic circle **AmE**

3 Match the prepositions to the correct diagrams.

1 over   2 under   3 between   4 along
5 past   6 through   7 around

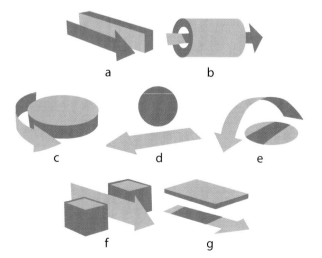

a   b

c   d   e

f   g

4 Look at the map in **1** and complete these sentences with a preposition from **3**.

1 The road to Fletchley goes .... the railway line.
2 The motorway goes .... the railway line.
3 The railway line runs .... two television towers.
4 When you drive from Boxted to Redhill, you pass .... Hockley.
5 You drive .... a church on your way from Boxted to Hockley.
6 The road to Andridge goes .... the river.
7 There are a lot of trees .... Lake Foss.

5 Complete these instructions for getting from Foss to Fletchley. Use the words in the list.

~~towards~~	exit	along	miss	off
signposted	after	under	right	past

Head north _towards_ Crockley. Just ....¹ you go through Crockley, you'll come to a roundabout. Take the first ....². It's ....³ to Bletcham. Turn ....⁴ at the traffic lights in Bletcham and join the motorway. Go ....⁵ the motorway for about five miles and you'll go ....⁶ two television towers on the right. Get ....⁷ the motorway at the next exit. Go through the tunnel ....⁸ the railway line and you'll come to Fletchley. You can't ....⁹ it!

6 Play a game with the class. Make two teams. Each team writes directions from the room you're in now to another place. Take turns to read your directions to the other team. The other team listens and says what place it is.

7 Work with a partner.

A – look at the information below.
B – look at file 27 on page 111.

A

You are at the airport and you need to get to your partner's factory. Your map is old and out of date. Ask your partner how to get there and draw the route on your map. (Use the grid boxes to help you.)

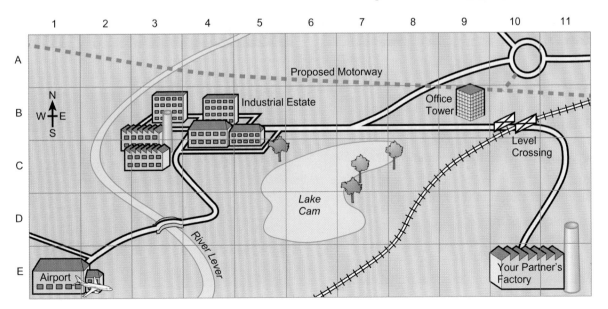

Getting around

1 (13.2) What do you think these people are saying?
Listen to the travellers asking and answering questions.
Match each conversation to the correct photograph.

a

b

c

d

2 (13.2) Listen to conversation 1 again.

1 Does the bill include tax and service?
2 How will the customer pay the tip?
3 What's wrong with the bill?
4 What else does the customer need?

3 Read the menu. Find the names of:

1 two types of fruit
2 three types of meat
3 four types of vegetable.

Brainstorm the names of more fruits, meats, and vegetables.

Menu

Dish of the day:
* T-bone steak
  - best Scottish beef
  - comes with a
    green salad
Home-made soups
* Chicken
* Asparagus

Pizzas
* Mushroom
* Ham

Side dishes
* French fries
* Tomato and onion
  salad

Desserts
* Apple pie
* Ice cream
  - strawberry,
    vanilla, and
    chocolate

4 Who could say these things in a restaurant: a waiter or a customer?

1 Here's the menu.
2 Can you tell me what this is?
3 What can you recommend?
4 Would you like a starter?
5 I'll have the salmon for my main course.
6 How would you like your steak cooked?

5 Work with a partner.

A – you are waiter in a restaurant.
B – you are a customer. Order a meal and pay the bill.

6 (13.2) Listen to conversation 2 again and complete the questions.

1 Did you .... these bags yourself?
2 Has anyone .... you anything to carry?
3 And have you .... them with you the .... time .... you packed?
4 Are you .... any knives or sharp instruments?
5 Do you have any .... with you?

7 Use the questions in **6** to act out the conversation with a partner.

A – you are the security guard.
B – you are the passenger.

8 (13.2) Listen to conversation 3 again. Are these statements true (T) or false (F)?

1 The bus goes to Heathrow.
2 The man wants to go to terminal 4.
3 He buys a return ticket for £18.15.
4 The bus driver can't give him change.
5 The bus will get there at around 4.30.
6 The driver will tell him when they arrive.

Asking people to repeat

If you don't hear, you can say *Could you say that again?* or simply *Sorry?*
You can also be more specific:
Sorry, where does it go? How much was that?

9 Practise asking someone to repeat information. Work with a partner. Take turns to ask specific questions about the information in **bold**. Use the phrases in the list.

how much	where	how far	why
what time	how long	how many	

Example
A *This bus goes to Gatwick.*
B *Sorry, where does it go?*
A *Gatwick.*

1 This bus goes to **Gatwick**.
2 It leaves at **2.30**.
3 It'll take **a couple of hours**.
4 Gatwick's about **60 miles**.
5 We'll make **three** stops.
6 A single ticket's **£16.50**.
7 I can't give you change, **because I don't carry it**.

10 (13.2) Listen to conversation 4 again.

1 What's the price?
2 What does it include?
3 What's CDW?
4 What happens if she has an accident?

Checking understanding

We often check information by:
– asking more questions: *What's CDW? Does that mean ...?*
– repeating things ourselves: *Did you say ...? So that's ... then?*

11 Work with a partner.
A – look at the information below.
B – look at file 5 on page 103.

A – ask your partner what these abbreviations mean and check you understand. Try to use the phrases in the box.

1 PIN
2 VAT
3 ID
4 WC
5 ATM
6 ZIP

Dimensions

1 Where is the Great Sphinx and how old is it?
Is it hollow or solid? Read the text and find out.

The mystery of the Sphinx

The Great Sphinx is 20 m high. Its body is more than 74 m long and its face is 6 m wide. Many scientists think it was built with the Egyptian pyramids 4,500 years ago. But the pyramids have horizontal marks on their surface caused by wind erosion, and there are some vertical marks on the surface of the Sphinx. Some scientists think they were caused by water erosion. If they are correct, the Sphinx is much older – perhaps 7,000–9,000 years old.

In the 1840s, someone drilled a hole behind the Sphinx's head. The hole went down over eight metres and the Sphinx's body was solid rock. But in 1993, a German engineer put a small robot with a camera inside another small hole. It travelled 60 m along a small tunnel taking photographs and he believes there was a secret door at the end. The Sphinx probably weighs over 200 tonnes. That's extremely heavy. Only three or four cranes in the world are large enough to lift 200 tonnes today, so some people think the Sphinx was built by aliens.

2 Here are some statements about the Sphinx. Are they facts (F) or opinions (O)?

1 The Sphinx is twenty metres high. ......
2 The Sphinx was built at the same time as the pyramids. ......
3 The Sphinx has vertical marks on its surface. ......
4 The vertical marks were caused by water erosion. ......
5 The Sphinx is seven to nine thousand years old. ......
6 There's a secret door inside the Sphinx. ......
7 Only three or four cranes can lift 200 tonnes today. ......
8 The Sphinx was built by aliens. ......

3 Complete these statistics.

1 Height ....
2 Length ....
3 Face width ....
4 Weight ....
5 Age ....
6 Hole depth ....
7 Tunnel length ....

Depth

We use *depth* to talk about how far down, in, or out something goes.
The depth of the swimming pool = how far down it goes
The depth of a hole in the wall = how far inside it goes
The depth of a bookcase = how far it sticks out from the wall

4 Complete these questions about the statistics in **3**.

1 How *high* is the Sphinx?
2 How .... is it?
3 How .... is its face?
4 How .... is it?
5 How .... is it?
6 How .... is the hole?
7 How .... is the tunnel?

Think of other ways to ask these questions.

Example
How high is it? – What's its height?

5 Work with a partner. Look at the statistics in **3** and ask and answer questions.

Example
A *How high is the Sphinx?*
B *It's 20 m high.*

tall and high

We usually use *tall* for long, thin things like people, trees, and buildings with many floors. We use *high* for other things, like mountains and walls.

6 Complete the sentences with *high* or *tall*.

1 Mount Everest is 8,848 metres ....
2 There is a .... tree outside my window.
3 How .... are you?
4 The sun is .... in the sky.
5 The castle was built on .... ground.
6 There are a lot of .... skyscrapers in Manhattan.

7 Work with a partner.

A – look at the information below.
B – look at file 23 on page 110.
A
Ask questions to complete this information. Answer your partner's questions.

Example
How long is the Eurotunnel?

· .... miles long
· Has two rail tunnels and one service tunnel

The Eurotunnel, between England and France

· .... years old
· The small stones weigh about four tons
· The large stones weigh about .... tons

Stonehenge, England

· .... m tall
· 320.75 m tall with the antennae
· Weighs .... tons (including 40 tons of paint)

The Eiffel Tower, Paris

· 450 ft high
· Each side is .... ft long

The Great Pyramid, Giza, Egypt

· More than 2000 years old
· Over .... kilometres long
· You can see it from the moon

The Great Wall, China

· .... tall
· Two towers. Each tower has 88 floors
· Together they have .... windows

The Petronas Towers, Kuala Lumpur, Malaysia

Quantities

1 Do you ever take part in teleconferences? These pictures show an experiment in three-dimensional teleconferencing at the University of North Carolina. It's called tele-immersion. How do you think it works?

2 Complete this description of the two pictures. Use *is*, *are*, *isn't*, and *aren't*.

In both pictures, there .... ¹ a lot of pictures on the walls and there .... ² some electrical equipment on the ceiling. There .... ³ any windows, so there .... ⁴ much light. The office above looks smaller. There .... ⁵ just one person and there .... ⁶ nothing behind the desk. But in the bottom picture there .... ⁷ three people behind the desk and there .... ⁸ more space.

When do we say *there is* and when do we say *there are*? Which form do we use with:

1 singular countable nouns – *a person, a desk*?
2 plural countable nouns – *people, pictures*?
3 uncountable nouns – *space, equipment*?

3 (14.1) Listen to some people talking about tele-immersion and find out how it works.

4 Work with a partner.

1 How many people are really in the office?
2 How is tele-immersion different to tele-conferencing?
3 What's unusual about the glasses?
4 Why isn't there much light?
5 What's on the ceiling?
6 What's the best thing about tele-immersion?
7 Would you like to communicate with people via tele-immersion? Why / Why not?

5 (14.1) Complete the words in these sentences, then listen again to check your answers.

1 How m.......... people can you see?
2 There isn't m.......... light.
3 We have to control the light. We still have a l.......... work to do on that, but there's e.......... light to see what you're doing.
4 We use a l.......... of cameras and projectors. You can see a f.......... of them on the ceiling.
5 We can use walls, tables – so we have p.......... of space to display information.

6 Complete the rule with *countable* and *uncountable*.

much, many, a little, a few
We use *many* with .... nouns. *How many people can you see?*
We use *much* with .... nouns. *There isn't much light.*
We use *a little* with .... nouns. *We have a little more work to do.*
We use *a few* with .... nouns. *You can see a few cameras.*

7 Choose the correct word.

1 Could I have a *little/few* help?
2 How *much/many* money do you have on you?
3 Only a *little/few* of our products are made from recycled materials.
4 There aren't *many/much* suppliers who can make this part.
5 These plants are dying. Can you give them a *little/few* water?
6 We don't have *much/many* paper left. Can you order some more?
7 We only need a *little/few* minutes to get ready.
8 How *much/many* windows does your office have?

Talking about quantities

Much and *many* are common in questions and negatives.
How much time do we have?
There aren't many people here.

In positive sentences we usually say *a lot of* (or *lots of*), *plenty of*, or *enough*. We can use these expressions with countable and uncountable nouns.
We have lots of equipment and a lot of spare parts.
We have plenty of ideas, but we don't have enough time.

Enough means 'as much / many as necessary'.
Plenty means 'enough and more'.

8 Work with a partner. Find out about each other's workplaces. What do you have plenty of and what don't you have enough of? Begin:

Is there much / a lot of / plenty of / enough …?
Are there many / a lot of / plenty of / enough …?

Ask about:
1 people
2 space to work
3 noise
4 quiet places to work
5 cubicles
6 Internet connections
7 electronic equipment
8 computer hardware
9 security cameras
10 fire extinguishers
11 storage space
12 windows
13 fresh air
14 daylight
15 plants
16 time to relax

Example
A *Are there a lot of people where you work?*
B *No, there aren't many.*
A *Is there enough space to work?*
B *Yes, there's plenty.*

9 Work with some other students and design your perfect workspace.

1 Make a list of all the things you need to be really happy and productive – equipment, fresh air, music, etc.
2 Draw a plan of the workspace, showing where everything will go, and prepare some sentences about your picture. Use all of these words at least once: *plenty, enough, much, many, a lot, a few, a little.*
3 Show your plan to the class and describe it. Explain why it's perfect for you.

15 *What's the schedule?*

Making arrangements

1 (15.1) Two people are organizing a product demonstration. Listen and write down the dates and times they arrange to meet.

	When?
1 Planning meeting	
2 Sales meeting	
3 Practice of the product demo	
4 Product demo	

2 (15.1) Complete the words below, then listen again and check your answers.

1 When are you f..........?
2 I'm t.......... u.......... this week. Next week's better.
3 Can we finish b.......... twelve?
4 Yes, two hours s.......... be long enough.
5 How long will that t..........? About an hour?
6 How a.......... Thursday 15th at two o'clock?
7 I can't m.......... two, but I can m.......... three.
8 OK, let's s.......... three o'clock t...........
9 Let's make a note of it and we can c.......... it later.
10 I don't think I can. I'm very s.......... of time.
11 I'm o.......... holiday* then. I'm not back u.......... the twenty-sixth.

holiday **BrE** – vacation **AmE**

3 Find words and expressions in **2** that mean:

1 busy
2 not later than a particular time
3 up to a particular time

> ### *by* and *until*
>
> We use **by** to say something will happen at or before a certain time.
> *Can we finish **by** 12 o'clock?* (Not later than 12. Possibly before 12.)
>
> We use **until** to say something will continue up to a certain time.
> *I'm not back **until** the 26th.* (I come back on the 26th – up to the 26th I'm away.)

4 Complete another conversation about the demo. Use *by* or *until*.

A Can we meet on the 15th to talk about the demo? Say three o'clock?
B I have a conference call at 2.30, so I won't be free ....¹ 3.30. Is that too late?
A No, 3.30 is fine.
B Can you send me the plans ....² Friday?
A No, I need to meet with Peter first and he's not free ....³ next week.
B Can you practise the demo next week?
A No, we'll have to wait ....⁴ Peter gets back from holiday.
B Will he be back ....⁵ the 26th?
A Yes, but he's not arriving ....⁶ the morning of the 26th. We need to start at 6.30 to be ready ....⁷ 9.00.
B But Peter will have to get up at 5 a.m. to be here ....⁸ 6.30.
A Too bad!

5 Complete these phrases for making arrangements. Use words from the list.

enough	make	let's	about	shall
confirm	won't	long	fine	take

Making arrangements

Suggesting times
How ....[1] the sixteenth?
Are you free next Tuesday?
..........[2] we meet around ten o'clock?

Saying yes
3.30 is ....[3].
Yes, I'm free then.
That's good for me.

Saying when you're available
I can't ....[4] ten o'clock, but I can manage eleven.
I ....[5] be free until 4.30.
I'm very short of time this week. Next week's better …

Estimating time
How ....[6] do we need?
How long will it ....[7]? Can we finish by twelve?
An hour should be long ....[8].

Confirming arrangements
..........[9] say Tuesday at three, then.
I'll meet you here at three o'clock.
Let's make a note of it and ....[10] it later.

6 Practise the phrases with a partner.

A – think of a job you want your partner to do.
B – think of some reasons why you're too busy to help your partner. Then follow the instructions below.

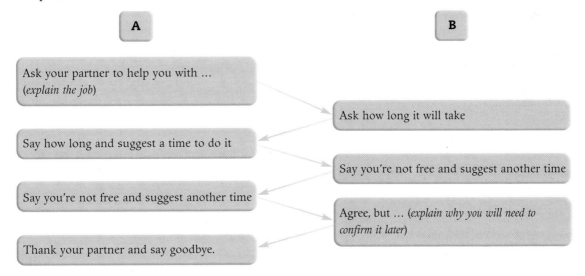

A

Ask your partner to help you with …
(*explain the job*)

Say how long and suggest a time to do it

Say you're not free and suggest another time

Thank your partner and say goodbye.

B

Ask how long it will take

Say you're not free and suggest another time

Agree, but … (*explain why you will need to confirm it later*)

7 Work with a partner.

A – look at file 29 on page 112.
B – look at file 37 on page 117.

Writing emails

1 Five people need help. Who do you think they are writing to – a colleague, a customer, a supplier, etc? Which emails are urgent?

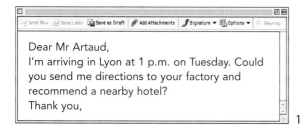

Dear Mr Artaud,
I'm arriving in Lyon at 1 p.m. on Tuesday. Could you send me directions to your factory and recommend a nearby hotel?
Thank you,

1

Hi Alex,
We have two urgent orders and one of our machining centres has broken down. Could you do some machining work for us? We'd really appreciate it.

2

Dear Mr Sousa,
We had a fire in our warehouse yesterday and it destroyed the last shipment of covers you sent us. We need another shipment immediately. How soon can you send them?
Many thanks,

3

Hello Tom,
Please give the attached order top priority. The sales department promised delivery by March 25th.
Tnx

4

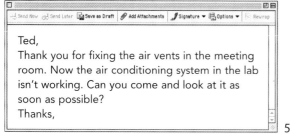

Ted,
Thank you for fixing the air vents in the meeting room. Now the air conditioning system in the lab isn't working. Can you come and look at it as soon as possible?
Thanks,

5

2 <u>Underline</u> the different words and phrases that are used in **1** to:

1 ask for help
2 say thank you.

Which expressions can you use with people you know well, and which are more formal?

3 Match these replies to the correct email in **1**.

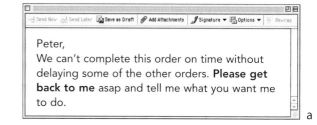

Peter,
We can't complete this order on time without delaying some of the other orders. **Please get back to me** asap and tell me what you want me to do.

a

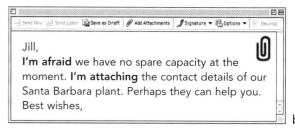

Jill,
I'm afraid we have no spare capacity at the moment. **I'm attaching** the contact details of our Santa Barbara plant. Perhaps they can help you.
Best wishes,

b

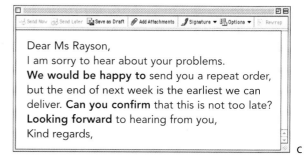

Dear Ms Rayson,
I am sorry to hear about your problems. **We would be happy to** send you a repeat order, but the end of next week is the earliest we can deliver. **Can you confirm** that this is not too late? **Looking forward** to hearing from you,
Kind regards,

c

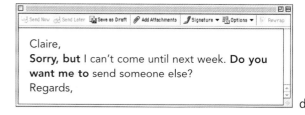

Claire,
Sorry, but I can't come until next week. **Do you want me to** send someone else?
Regards,

d

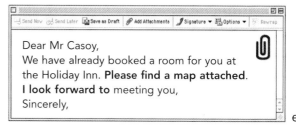

Dear Mr Casoy,
We have already booked a room for you at the Holiday Inn. **Please find a map attached.** **I look forward to** meeting you,
Sincerely,

e

4 Look at the phrases in **bold** in **3**. Find two phrases that:

1 introduce bad news
2 offer help
3 ask for a reply
4 refer to an attachment
5 refer to a future contact.

5 Complete the emails using expressions from the emails in **1** and **3**.

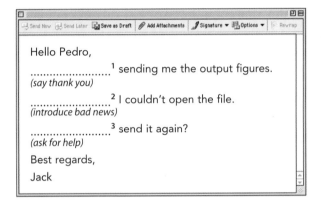

Hello Pedro,

.........................¹ sending me the output figures.
(say thank you)

.........................² I couldn't open the file.
(introduce bad news)

.........................³ send it again?
(ask for help)

Best regards,

Jack

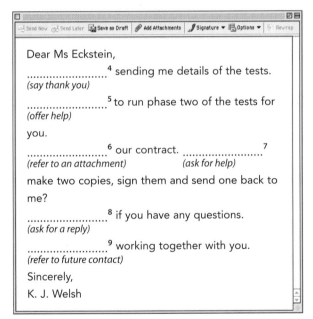

Dear Ms Eckstein,

.........................⁴ sending me details of the tests.
(say thank you)

.........................⁵ to run phase two of the tests for
(offer help)

you.

.........................⁶ our contract. ....⁷
(refer to an attachment)   *(ask for help)*

make two copies, sign them and send one back to me?

.........................⁸ if you have any questions.
(ask for a reply)

.........................⁹ working together with you.
(refer to future contact)

Sincerely,

K. J. Welsh

-ing forms

In some expressions we use *-ing* after a preposition (*for, to, in, at,* etc.).
Thank you for *fixing* the air vents.
Looking forward to *meeting* you.

6 Think of some different endings for these expressions. Use an *-ing* form.

1 Thank you for …
2 We're looking forward to …
3 We're interested in …
4 I never leave the office without …
5 Our company is very good at …
6 When this lesson finishes, how about …?

7 Think of some problems that slow things down in your workplace, for example, late deliveries, not enough production capacity, unreliable machinery, management changing its mind. Who can help you solve these problems – colleagues, suppliers, customers?

1 Work in pairs or small groups. Choose one of the problems and write a short email to someone asking for help. Explain:
   a what the problem is
   b what you want them to do and when.
2 One person should write and the other(s) should dictate and check spelling, etc.

Deliver your email to another group. Read the email you receive and write a reply.

Dimensions

1 What is *Aquarius*? Who lives on *Aquarius* and for how long? Would you like to live there? (Why / Why not?)

Aquarius is an underwater laboratory. It is made of steel and it can withstand pressures at ocean depths up to 36 metres. It is currently located in the Florida Keys National Marine Sanctuary at a depth of 19 metres. That is about four metres off the ocean floor.

It consists of a cylinder which is nearly three metres in diameter and attached to a base plate, so it stays at the bottom of the ocean. The laboratory weighs 73 tons and the base plate weighs 103 tons. Although it's only 13 metres long, six metres wide, and five metres high, six scientists and technicians can live in *Aquarius* for ten days, or even a month, and study underwater life. It has all the comforts of home: six bunk beds, a shower and toilet, hot water, a kitchen with a microwave and refrigerator, air conditioning, and computers with wireless connections.

A side view of Aquarius, before it was lowered into the ocean

2 Complete this chart.

AQUARIUS LABORATORY
Length
Width
Height
Weight
Cylinder diameter
Base plate weight
Current depth
Maximum depth of operations

3 Think of different ways to ask these questions about the dimensions.

What's the:

1 length of Aquarius?
   How long is Aquarius?
2 width of Aquarius?

   ....
3 height of Aquarius?

   ....
4 weight of Aquarius?

   ....
5 diameter of the cylinder?

   ....
6 current depth of Aquarius?

   ....
7 maximum depth of operations?

   ....

4 Work with a partner. Ask and answer all the questions.

Example
A *How long is Aquarius?*
B *Thirteen metres.*

Containers

1 Match the containers and units in the table to the correct picture.

Container	often made of	often contains
a bottle	glass, plastic	wine, ...[1]
b cup	china	coffee, tea
c box	cardboard, metal	..........[2], tools, controls, tissues
d sack	polythene, ...[3]	sand, cement
e bag	paper, plastic, cloth	rubbish, ...[4], air
f tank	..........[5], plastic	water, petrol
g tube	a ductile metal, plastic	..........[6], ointment
h crate	lightweight metal, plastic, ...[7]	things you're shipping, beer
i pallet	wood	things you're putting on top of one another or stacking
j can	aluminium*, tin	paint, ...[8], oil, food
k barrel	wood, metal	oil, beer, wine

Unit	often made of	shape
l roll	paper, ...[9], tape	like a cylinder
m bar	metal, gold, chocolate, soap	like a rectangular box
n lump	coal, sugar, clay, ... [10]	irregular
o plank	wood	..........[11]
p block	heavy things like concrete	with flat sides

aluminium **BrE** – aluminum **AmE**

2 Complete the table with words and phrases from the list. Think of more words to add to the table.

aluminium foil	wood	matches
toothpaste	water	fizzy drinks
long and flat	cloth	cheese
school books	metal	

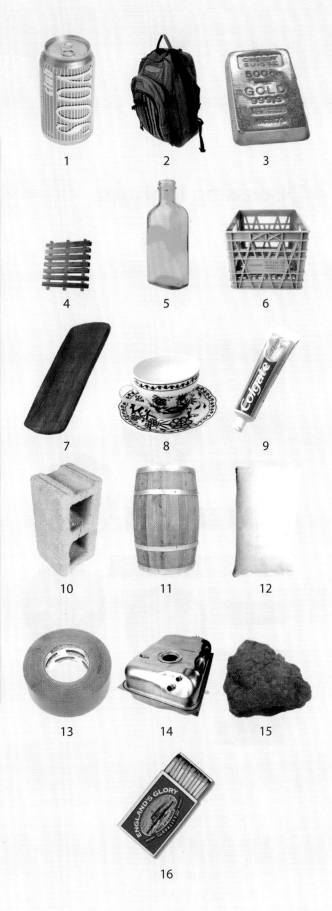

1

2

3

4

5

6

7

8

9

10

11

12

13

14

15

16

16 *What's the system?*

Discussing logistics

1 Which part of this supply chain focuses on:

1 storing and shipping goods?
2 buying materials?
3 selling products in shops?
4 production?

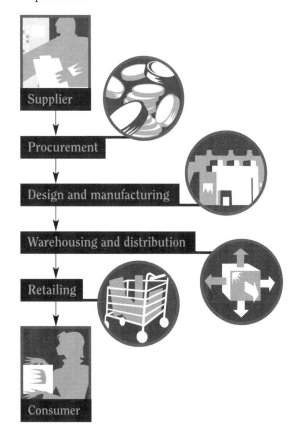

2 (16.1) You are going to hear four people who work in a different part of the supply chain. Listen and make a note of:

1 where they work
2 their job title
3 their biggest problem.

3 (16.1) Listen again and complete the sentences.

1 That's my job. I'm a ....
2 We .... some work to shipping companies.
3 Our biggest problem is keeping .... low.
4 We operate in a very ....
5 You have to listen very carefully to identify the market ....
6 My biggest problem is ....

4 Find the words and phrases in **3** which mean:

1 stocks of materials and goods
2 new movements and directions
3 the time from the beginning to the end of a manufacturing process
4 subcontract work to outside companies
5 someone who organizes supplies and services
6 an area or field of business where a lot of companies are operating.

5 English has many families of words that come from the same word root. Complete this table.

verbs	people	activities
to compete	competitor	competition
to produce		
	manufacturer	
		design
		shipping
to distribute		

Say the words in the table aloud. Where does the main stress fall?

manufacture ●●●●   *manufacturer* ●●●●●
manufacturing ●●●●●

In some word families, the main stress changes. Which ones?

6 Read about another company's supply chain. What's unusual about it?

Quick-Change Inventory

Most big fashion retailers have to guess what their customers will want in nine months' time so they can start making it now. But product cycle times are much shorter at Zara, a Spanish fashion company with 519 stores in 46 countries. It takes Zara just three weeks to go from designing a new product to selling it.

Zara is a complete supply chain, from start to finish. Design, manufacture, and distribution are integrated and they take place in-house. Zara's competitors outsource all the manufacturing and use cheaper foreign labour, but Zara makes half its clothes itself. It has 23 highly automated factories in Spain where the fabrics are cut and dyed by robots. Most finished products are only in its warehouse for a few hours. It doesn't store clothes. It moves them.

Zara can *respond* quickly to market trends. At the end of every working day the store managers report on sales to the headquarters in Spain. They give *feedback* about what customers like, and this information goes back to the design department right away. Product lines can be *discarded* or *altered* and new lines can be created immediately.

The company keeps costs down by keeping inventories low. New products are delivered to the stores twice a week and *lead times* are short. Zara can receive and ship an order almost as fast as a teenage customer can change his or her mind, and that's very important in the world of fashion. It's what keeps Zara ahead of its competitors. *Rapid* design, just-in-time production, and fast *stock turnover* are the keys to Zara's success.

7 Match the words and expressions in *italics* in the text to these meanings.

1 thrown out
2 very quick, fast
3 changed
4 react and do something
5 the rate at which goods are sold and replaced in a shop
6 information about something you've done, which tells you how good it is
7 the time between accepting an order and shipping it, or getting paid

Word partnerships

Some English words are made from two words joined together.
outsource, in-house, feedback
But there are also separate words that we often use together.
lead times, supply chain, just-in-time
Together these words form a fixed expression.

8 Find some words that often go together in the boxes and make some fixed expressions.

finished	labour
foreign	products
competitive	times
highly	market
raw	materials
market	automated
cycle	trends

Example
finished products

9 Work with a partner.

A – look at file 25 on page 110.
B – look at file 9 on page 104.

Recycling

1 How old is your car? What will happen to it when it gets too old to drive? Think of parts and materials from cars. Which ones can be recycled or reused?

2 🎧 (16.2) Listen to someone describing the process of recycling a car and check your answers.

3 🎧 (16.2) Listen again and say what they do with:

1 the air bags
2 the fluids
3 the parts that are in good working order
4 the parts for recycling
5 the glass
6 the car body
7 the mixture that's left over.

4 Complete the flow chart with words from the list.

> Draining Shredding Sorting Activating
> Burying Crushing Dismantling

5 When you *activate* air bags, you blow them up or fill them with air. Match the other verbs in the flow chart to the correct meaning.

1 pressing or squeezing something together very hard
2 making a liquid flow away, so something is dry
3 taking something apart
4 tearing or cutting something up into small pieces
5 putting something in a hole in the ground and covering it
6 putting things into different groups or places, so they are correctly organized

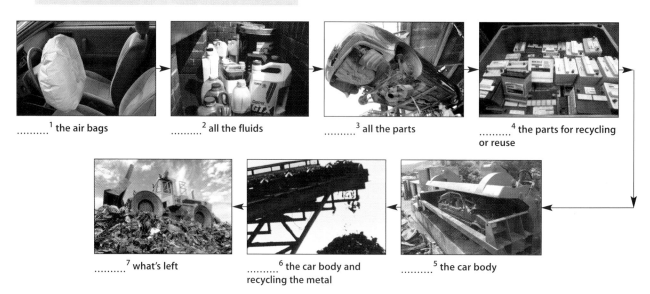

.... ¹ the air bags

.... ² all the fluids

.... ³ all the parts

.... ⁴ the parts for recycling or reuse

.... ⁷ what's left

.... ⁶ the car body and recycling the metal

.... ⁵ the car body

6 Work with a partner. Look at another flow chart and describe the process of recycling plastic milk bottles. Use these words and phrases: *First ... After that ... Then ... Next ... Finally ...*

Example
A *What happens first?*
B *First, they ...*
A *What happens after that?*
B *After that, they ...*

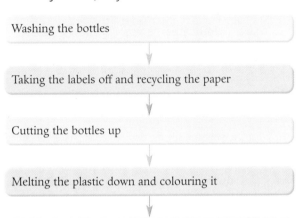

Washing the bottles

Taking the labels off and recycling the paper

Cutting the bottles up

Melting the plastic down and colouring it

Making the plastic into containers, pipes, car parts, and so on

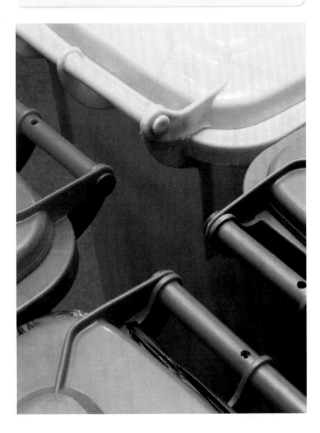

Two-part verbs

A lot of English verbs have two parts – a verb and a small word like *off, up, out, in, on*, etc. These verbs are common in informal spoken English.
We **take** the labels **off**.   Then we **cut** the plastic **up**.

There is often a more formal way of saying the same thing with one word.
We **remove** the labels.   Then we **shred** the plastic.

7 Find the two-part verbs in these sentences and match them to a word in the list.

| dismantle   fasten   inflate   connect |
| disconnect   drain   discard |

1 Blow the balloon up.
2 I'm going to take this radio apart.
3 It's wet. We need to pump the liquid out.
4 Be careful not to pull the cable out.
5 Throw the parts we don't need away.
6 Do the lid up tightly.
7 Can I plug my computer in here?

8 Draw a flow chart to show a process in your company. It can be any process you like, for example, a production process, a shipping process, an ordering process. Think about how you can explain it in English. When you are ready, work with a partner. Take turns describing and explaining your processes.

Attachments

1 What's this equipment for? What's it testing? Locate these things in the picture (a–j).

1 golf ball
2 golf driver
3 wheel
4 rope
5 string

6 air bag
7 turbine
8 bell
9 gauge
10 plunger

What other parts of the equipment can you name?

2 How does it work? What's the first action? Use these verbs to describe what happens.

| cuts | indicates | rings | hits | ~~pulls~~ |
| spins | escapes | pushes | turns | |

3 Use each verb once to complete this description.

When everyone is ready, the first technician ..*pulls*..[1] the string and .... [2] the bell. Then the second technician .... [3] the rope and the wheel .... [4] round. The golf driver .... [5] the ball at the plunger and .... [6] the plunger into the bag of air. Some air .... [7] and .... [8] the turbine. The gauge .... [9] the estimated distance of the shot.

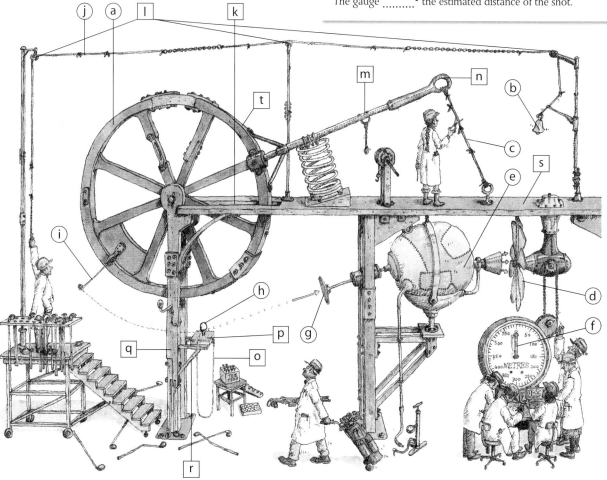

4 Read this description of the equipment. Locate the items in bold in the picture (k–t).

> The wheel rests on a vertical wooden **support** attached to a horizontal **platform**. There's a **slot** in the centre of the platform at one end, so the wheel can turn freely. A cylindrical wooden **beam** is bolted onto the **rim** of the wheel at right angles. The beam has a large **ring** at one end, which is tied to another ring on the platform. A piece of string runs over three **pulleys** above the machine. When someone pulls it, it rings a small bell. The golf ball is placed on a **shelf** supported by a wooden **bracket**. The ball is attached to the shelf by a thin metal **chain**.

5 Match these phrases to the best diagram.

1	is supported	6	is pivoted
2	is attached / stuck	7	is hinged
3	is secured with brackets	8	is linked / connected
4	is bolted	9	is housed
5	is tied	10	is clamped

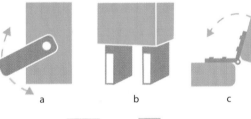

a   b   c

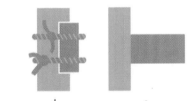

d   e

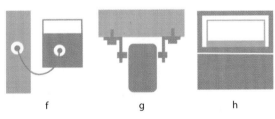

f   g   h

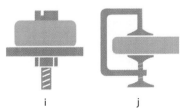

i   j

6 Draw three more diagrams for these phrases.

1 is suspended
2 is hooked
3 is chained

7 Look around the room and find some joints and places where things are fastened or connected. Describe the connections.

Example
The legs are bolted on to the frame of the table.

8 Work with a partner.

A – look at the information below.
B – look at file 32 on page 114.

A
You and your partner have the same picture, but they are incomplete.

1 Ask your partner how these things are connected, linked, etc., and draw the attachments on your picture.
   1 the television
   2 the dog
   3 the clock
   4 the torch
   5 the toothbrush and toothpaste

2 Tell your partner how other things are attached, supported, etc. so they can draw the attachments on their picture.

Locating parts

1 (17.1) Listen to someone ordering parts for this vacuum pump. Which parts does he want?

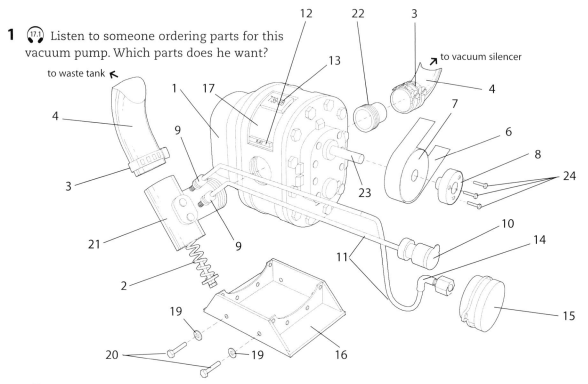

2 (17.1) Listen again and identify these parts. Write the part numbers in the table.

Part	Part number
a plate	
b serial number	
c model number	
d shaft	
e pulley	
f belt	
g flanged hub	
h hub screw	

3 (17.1) Listen again and complete these sentences.

1 Is it on the .... of the pump?
2 No, it's on the ...., near the ....
3 The model number is .... that, near the .... of the plate somewhere.
4 Well, ... the pump, there's a rod that sticks out.
5 No, but .... the pulley there's another circular part.

4 Compare these locations:

*The shaft is **on the front of** the pump.*
*The pulley is **in front of** the pump.*

Which phrase do we use when things aren't touching?

Describe where things are in relation to the television. Use phrases from the list.

behind	on the front of	under
in front of	on the bottom of	above
on the top of	on the back of	

The remote control is in front of the television.

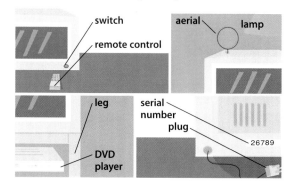

5 Read this description of the pump. Identify more parts and write their part numbers in the table.

> The valve assembly screws into the left hand side of the pump. It is connected to the waste tank by a hose. A circular clamp fits round the hose and holds it securely. The spring relief valve sticks out of the bottom of the valve assembly.
>
> Two connectors fit into two holes on the front of the valve assembly. They are attached to two long tubes. The top tube leads to the elbow joint and the vacuum gauge. The bottom tube leads to the lubricating cup.
>
> A large outlet nipple screws into the right hand side of the pump. It's connected to the vacuum silencer by a hose. Two clamps fit round the hose and hold it securely.
>
> The pump sits on top of the mount. There are two holes in the left hand side of the mount. Two bolts pass through the holes and fasten the pump to the mount. The bolts pass through two washers.

Part		Part number
a	valve assembly	21
b	hose	
c	clamp	
d	spring relief valve	
e	connector	
f	tube	
g	elbow joint	
h	vacuum gauge	
i	lubricating cup	
j	outlet nipple	
k	mount	
l	bolt	
m	washer	

6 Look at the diagram in **1** and use the phrases in the list to complete these sentences.

~~is connected to~~	screws into	fit into
sticks out of	leads to	
passes through	fits round	

Example
One of the hoses is connected to the waste tank.

1 The other hose .... the vacuum silencer.
2 The valve assembly .... the pump.
3 The shaft .... the pump.
4 The shaft .... the pulley.
5 The belt .... the pulley.
6 The connectors .... the holes.

7 Work with a partner.

A – look at the information below.
B – look at file 35 on page 115.

A
This diagram shows an ice-making machine, but five of the part names are missing. Your partner has the same diagram. Find out the names of the missing parts and write them down.

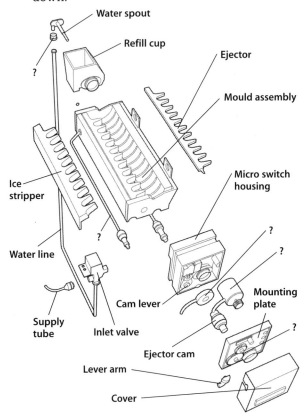

18 *Which is better?*

Comparing benefits

1 Think of some places where robots are used. What are they used for? Does your company use robots? (What for?) Read these two stories about robots and answer the questions.

> Peter Knigge used to get up early every morning to milk the cows on his farm in Wisconsin, USA. Then he bought two robots. Now the robots milk the cows three times a day. That's more often than Peter could milk them, so the cows produce 10 per cent more milk and the farm is more productive. But the best thing is that Peter can stay in bed later in the mornings.

    1 Is milk production higher or lower?
    2 Is Peter getting up earlier or later?

> The Japanese company NEC used robots to assemble its mobile phones. Then it found that it could do the job more efficiently if it used people. 'Using robots was good, but now we're discovering that using people for multi-task work is faster', said Mr Saitama, the company president. NEC now uses people and assembles the phones 45 per cent faster.

    1 Were the robots good at the job?
    2 Who assembled the phones more efficiently: robots or people?

Comparing how we do things

Use *more / less* + adverb.
*People do the job **more efficiently**.*
*Robots do the job **less efficiently**.*

Irregular forms: *well,* **better**   *badly,* **worse**
                      fast, **faster**   *hard,* **harder**
                      early, **earlier**   *late,* **later**

2 Complete these sentences. Use a comparative adverb.

We operated efficiently before, but with our new computer system <u>we operate more efficiently</u>.

  1 This machine prints fast, but the new machine ....
  2 My car ran well before, but after the engine tune up, it ....
  3 This blade cuts badly, but that rusty old blade ....
  4 I get up early most mornings, but I have more jobs to do on Mondays so I ....
  5 I drive carefully, but my wife ....
  6 We finished work late today, but yesterday we ....
  7 My boss works hard, but I ....

3 What kind of robot is this advertisement for? Why does the human guard have lots of equipment? What kind of equipment is it?

a) Locates things he cannnot see with radar
b) Detector for smoke and other dangers
c) Gas detector
d) Continuous recording
e) Equipped for low lighting
g) Data logging
f) Continuous status reporting
h) Energy for a 12-hour patrol

$16/hour + annual pay increase (not including equipment)

4 Label the equipment. Write the letters in the boxes.

1 wall-penetrating radar ☐
2 a laptop computer ☐
3 an environmental monitoring system ☐
4 a video camera ☐
5 night-vision lenses ☐
6 a microphone ☐
7 a bird in a cage ☐
8 lots of chocolate bars ☐

5 Read about some of the things the Sentrybot does. Can the human guard do the same things?

- Sees in poor light
- Makes continuous status reports
- Quickly detects smoke and other danger
- Detects gas fast
- Accurately logs data
- Records everything it sees
- Sees through solid walls
- Patrols continuously for 12 hours at a time

Reliable protection from Sentrybot

It's a little too good to be human.

$15/hour first 12 months
$2.00 an hour after that
(includes maintenance and installation)

6 Work with a partner. Ask and answer questions about the human guard. Use the information in **5**.

A *Can he see in poor light?*
B *Yes, he can. He has night-vision lenses.*
A *Can he make continuous status reports?*
B *Yes, he can. He has …*

7 The Sentrybot can do the same things as the human guard, but which one is better? Do you agree (A) or disagree (D) with these statements?

❶ You can patrol a warehouse more cheaply with human guards.

❷ It doesn't matter if a robot gets damaged. But if a human guard gets injured, it's more serious.

❸ A robot moves more slowly than a human guard.

❹ Human guards are less reliable than robots.

❺ Robots work harder than human guards.

❻ It takes longer to program a robot than it takes to train a human guard.

❼ A human guard has a better memory than a robot.

❽ A robot is more flexible and adaptable than a human.

❾ You can patrol a warehouse more efficiently with robots than with human guards.

❿ A robot isn't as intelligent as a human being.

Compare your opinions with some other students. Do you agree?

Weighing alternatives

1 Which is the most difficult issue in your job?

1 Time – meeting deadlines and avoiding delays

2 Quality – meeting specifications and avoiding mistakes

3 Cost – keeping to budget and finding ways to save money

2 (18.1) Listen to three different conversations. What problems are the people trying to solve? Are they worried about time, quality, or cost?

3 (18.1) Listen again and answer these questions.

Conversation 1
1 What's the problem with the gears?
2 Why can't they use plastic gears?
3 What do they decide to do?

Conversation 2
4 What's wrong with the fuel pump?
5 Why can't they buy another one?
6 Why can't they replace the system?

Conversation 3
7 What's the hold-up with the parts list?
8 What'll happen if they get another server?
9 What's the easiest solution?

Possibilities

After *if* we usually use the Present Simple to talk about the future.
If we **get** another server, it'll help. (NOT ~~If we will get another server~~)

What are we going to do if it **breaks down** again? (NOT ~~if it will break down~~)

4 Use the correct form of the verbs in the list to complete these sentences.

upgrade	be	work	have
outsource	use	cut	~~break down~~

Example
I'll call an engineer if the pump breaks down again.

1 If we .... some work, we can do the job faster.
2 I'll look into it next week if I .... time.
3 If we .... the software, it'll speed things up.
4 If we .... cheaper materials, we won't meet the specs.
5 I've changed the fuse, but I'll be surprised if it ....
6 We won't be able to replace the part if it .... obsolete.
7 If we .... some corners, we can save some money.

5 Discuss these time, quality, and cost questions with a partner and explain your answers.

Example
The easiest way to cook an egg is to boil it. If you don't boil it, you'll have to do more washing up.

1 What's the easiest way to cook an egg?
2 What's the most economical way to heat a house?
3 What's the most environmentally friendly way for you to get to work?
4 What's the safest way to pick up a heavy box?
5 What's the simplest way to open a jar with a tight lid?
6 What's the most effective way to remove blood stains from a shirt?
7 What's the best way to back up data on your PC?
8 What's the quickest way to get rich?

6 You are going to hold a meeting to solve some problems.

1 THE OIL TANK OUTSIDE THE ASSEMBLY SHOP
The tank is cracked and oil is leaking into the ground.

2 OFFICE TEMPERATURES
Your offices get too hot in summer and too cold in winter.

3 CAR PARKING
Local residents are complaining they can't park anywhere near your company during the day.

4 FORK-LIFT TRUCK ACCIDENTS
Five of your employees have been seriously injured by fork-lift trucks in the last three months.

5 QUEUES* IN THE CANTEEN
Too many people are going for lunch between 12.00 and 12.30. There aren't enough tables and people are standing in queues for ten minutes or more.

6 EMPLOYEES' LEVEL OF ENGLISH
Your company repairs and services engines. The manuals are all in English, but most of your employees can't understand them.

7 THE STRIKE
There is a railway strike so you cannot ship your products to your customers by rail. Your warehouse is full.

8 THE BIKE SHED
You are going to build a shed for your employees' bicycles, scooters, and motorbikes. You need to decide what materials to use.

9 COCKROACHES
There are cockroaches in the staff restrooms. You need to get rid of them and stop them returning.

queues **BrE** – lines **AmE**

1 Before you begin, read the problems and brainstorm some different ways to solve them. Think of solutions that:
   a are cheap
   b are quick and easy to do
   c will last a long time or are the best solution.

2 Decide which solutions you think are the best and prepare to explain why. Then work in a group with some other students. Hold the meeting and decide what to do about each problem.

7 Think of a time, quality, or cost problem you have at work. In small groups describe it to the other students. They should ask questions and suggest solutions.

Joints

1 Suggest different ways to join or fasten together two:

1 chains
2 pieces of paper
3 wires
4 pieces of wood
5 ends of a rope
6 copper pipes
7 pieces of cloth
8 bricks.

chains: You could insert a link, or join them together with a padlock.

And how could you unfasten them or take them apart?

2 Think of different ways to attach or fix:

1 a heavy mirror to a wall
2 a curtain in front of a window
3 a ceramic tile to a wall
4 a boat to a tree on the land
5 a piece of paper to a noticeboard
6 a wheel to a car
7 a piece of metal to a hole in the body of your car.

Action verbs

1 Match the verbs to the best diagram. Write the square number.

1 lift / raise Y33
2 lower ......
3 drop ......
4 cut ......
5 turn ......
6 rotate ......
7 weigh ......
8 transport ......
9 chain ......
10 lock ......
11 crush ......
12 squeeze ......
13 spin ......
14 paint ......
15 dip ......
16 pack ......
17 heat ......
18 discard / throw away ......
19 stack ......
20 inspect ......
21 shred ......
22 drain ......
23 bury ......
24 press / push ......

2 Work with a partner. Take turns to test each other.

A *What's Y33?*
B *It's 'raise'.*

	E	J	Y	I	G	H
3						
13						
30						
33						

Body parts

1 Label the creature with words from the list.

bottom	neck	arms	head	legs	lip
mouth	nose	back	body	foot	jaws
hands	face	teeth	elbow	tail	

2 We often use the names of these body parts to describe other physical structures. Use each word from **1** once to complete the text.

 This chair has two ....¹ and four ....². If you look at it from below, you see its ....³, and if you look at it from behind, you see its ....⁴.

 This joint bends in the middle, just like a human arm, so we call it an ....⁵ joint.

 This vice has two ....⁶, which can grip things.

 And this saw cuts with its ....⁷.

 We say we're at the ....⁸ of a ladder when we're at the bottom.

 The thin pointed end of this arrow is its ....⁹.

 But the thin pointed end of an aeroplane* is its ....¹⁰. Its ....¹¹ is at the rear.

 The narrow part of this bottle is the ....¹² and the hole where it opens is its ....¹³.

 Bottles and other hollow containers also have a ....¹⁴ at their edge.

 This clock has a ....¹⁵ and two ....¹⁶ to indicate the time.

 And finally, don't forget the word ....¹⁷. We use it to describe a whole structure or the main part of something, such as a car.

aeroplane **BrE** – airplane **AmE**

3 Think of more things we can describe with these words.

Examples
the arm of a crane, the leg of a table

4 Work in groups. Can you solve these riddles?

Example
What can be right, but can never be wrong?
Answer: an angle

1 What has a neck, but doesn't have a head?

2 What has two hands and a face, but no arms or legs?

3 What has a mouth and a fork, but cannot eat?

4 What has heads and tails, but doesn't have legs?

5 What has a foot but no head?

The answers are in file 11 on page 104.

Inventions

1 Leonardo da Vinci invented these things. What are they? Do they remind you of any modern inventions?

2 Read this text. Which sketch does it refer to specifically?

Sketches of these inventions were drawn in the fifteenth century by Leonardo da Vinci and although his sketch books contains many inventions, very few were built in his lifetime. He was interested in flying and he drew a lot of different flying machines, including this one with a rotating airscrew. It was powered by a wound-up spring and it works in a similar way to a modern helicopter. But the world's first helicopter wasn't built until many centuries later. The first helicopter that could carry a person was designed and flown by Paul Cornu in 1907.

Past passive

We form the past passive with *was* or *were* and the past participle.
*These sketches **were drawn** in the fifteenth century.*
*The first helicopter **wasn't built** until centuries later.*

We can use *by* to say what or who performed an action:
*It was powered **by** a wound-up spring.*
*It was designed **by** Paul Cornu.*

But often *by* is not necessary.
The first helicopter was flown in 1907.
Few inventions were built.

3 Complete these texts about the other sketches in **1**. Use *was* or *were* and the correct form of the verb in brackets. Which sketch does each text refer to?

1 The world's first successful parachute jump *was made* (make) from the top of a tower in France in 1783. But a device that looks similar to a modern skydiving parachute .... (draw) by Leonardo back in 1485.

2 Leonardo understood a lot about flight. For example, he understood that if landing gear .... (not fold up), it could slow down a plane. So he designed retractable landing gear for a plane that didn't exist. The first aeroplane with retractable landing gear .... (build) in 1933.

3 Several diving suits .... (design) by Leonardo, but one was special because the divers .... (not connect) to the surface of the water by tubes. They could swim freely and breathe the air in the suit. And in 1943, the world's first AquaLung® .... (develop) by Emile Gagnon and the film director Jacques-Yves Cousteau. It looked very similar.

4 Leonardo's military inventions included one for an armoured vehicle. It had wheels that .... (turn) by four soldiers who sat inside and rotated cranks. The first time tanks .... (use) was in 1917 in Cambrai, France, during World War I.

4 Work with a partner.

1 Where was the world's first successful parachute jump made?
2 What was built in 1933?
3 Who developed the AquaLung®?
4 When were tanks first used?

Passive questions

The AquaLung® was developed by Cousteau.
    ↑   ↑
What was developed?   **Who** developed the AquaLung®?

It was developed in France in 1943.
               ↑   ↑
    Where was it developed?   **When** was it developed?

---

5 Ask passive questions about these inventions.

1 *The video cassette recorder* was invented by *the Sony Corporation*.
2 It was invented in *Japan* in *1969*.
3 *The world's first parking meters* were installed in *Oklahoma City* in *1935*.
4 The meters weren't popular. Some were destroyed by *the town's citizens*.

6 Work with a partner.

A – look at the information below.
B – look at file 3 on page 102.

A
1 Read the information on some more inventions. Can you guess any of the missing information?
2 Ask your partner questions and complete the missing information.

Example
When was the telephone invented?

1	The telephone was invented by Alexander Graham Bell in .... (*when?*)
2	The ballpoint pen was invented by Ladislo Biro in 1938.
3	.... (*what?*) was invented by the Aztecs in Central America over fifteen hundred years ago.
4	Fibre optics were invented in India in 1955.
5	Jeans were invented by .... (*who?*) in 1873.
6	The first successful aeroplane* flight was made by the Wright Brothers in 1903.
7	Paper was invented .... (*where?*) around 105.
8	Teabags were invented by Thomas Sullivan in 1904.

aeroplane **BrE** – airplane **AmE**

Progress updates

1 What have you done so far today? Have you:

1 done any work?
2 spoken to anyone on the phone?
3 sent any emails?
4 had anything to eat?

Is there anything you haven't had time to do yet?

2 🎧 Listen to a conversation about three repair jobs. What are the jobs? Have they been done or not? Make notes in the chart.

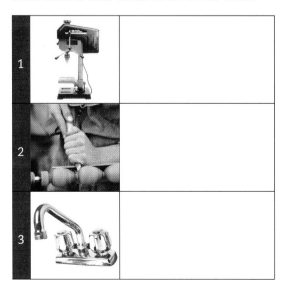

3 🎧 Listen again and complete the sentences.

1 .... you .... the drilling machine yet?
2 There .... a loose connection. I .... it and it's fine now.
3 I need a new part. I .... it yesterday and it should be here tomorrow.
4 And your wife .... me this morning.
5 She wants me to look at it. I ....
  time today, but I'll call by tomorrow.

Present Perfect and Past Simple

We use the Present Perfect to talk about recent actions.
I've repaired the machine.
Have you fixed it?

The time is indefinite. We mean 'some time up to now'.
I haven't had time today (at any time today, up to now).

We use the Past Simple to talk about actions that happened at a definite time.
I ordered the part yesterday.
Your wife called me this morning.

We can think of a definite time, even when we don't say the time.
I soldered it. (when I fixed it)
What was wrong with it? (before you fixed it)

4 Complete these sentences with the correct form of the word in brackets. Use the Present Perfect or Past Simple.

1 .... you .... these statistics recently? (update)
2 The machining centre .... three times last week. (break down)
3 Oh dear. I think I .... a screw. (lose)
4 I .... alongside a lot of good engineers in my life. (work)
5 We .... this measuring machine three years ago. (buy)
6 When .... the parts ....? (arrive)
7 .... you .... any samples recently? (take)
8 When I found the loose connection, I .... the wires. (solder)
9 Who is that man in workshop 2? I .... him before. (not see)

5 Work with a partner.

A – look at the notes below.
B – look at file 36 on page 116.

A

1 You are the supervisor. Last Monday, you gave your partner this list of jobs to do. You want to know how they are getting on. Read the list and prepare questions to ask.

Have you fixed / checked / investigated the ...?
What was wrong with it / them?

6 Prepare to update another student on your progress at work.

1 Write a list of your jobs. Include some things that you've done recently and some things that you need to do. Mix them up.

2 Exchange your list with another student and take turns to ask and answer questions about them.

Have you fixed the generator yet?
No, we haven't. The parts we need haven't arrived yet.

JOB	
1 Fix energy saving lamp in reception	Perhaps the transformer is broken?
2 Investigate the complaint about heating system in Workshop 6B	Problem adjusting temperature
3 Replace the damaged safety guard on milling machine in Workshop 2	New guard delivered last Friday
4 Inspect high voltage cable in Workshop 6B	
5 Rewire the plug on the production manager's desk lamp	He doesn't know how to do it.

2 Ask your partner about their progress. Find out if there are any problems.

3 Now change roles. Your partner is your supervisor. He / She gave you this list of jobs to do last Monday. Read the jobs and get ready to tell your partner what you have done.

JOB	
1 Check the air tools	Air supply OK but replaced 3 leaking hoses. Tuesday 3pm.
2 Find out why the grinding machine is making a funny noise	Wednesday 12.30 am. Looked at it. No idea what's wrong.
3 Repair the leaking pipe in Workshop 4A	Fixed Thursday 10.45 am. No problem!
4 Check the oil and air filters on compressor A-96	Replaced air filters. Need to order oil filters.
5 The showerhead in my apartment is blocked. Please look at it if you get time.	Replaced showerhead Friday 2 pm. Cindy has some more jobs she wants me to do.

4 Answer your partner's questions and tell them about your progress.

20 *What's it made of?*

Materials

1 Brainstorm things that can be made of these materials.

> steel, leather, rubber, fibreglass, nylon, gold, cardboard, wool, ceramic, wood, plastic, polystyrene*, glass, wax, paper, polythene, foam rubber, cotton, aluminium*

polystyrene **BrE** – styrofoam **AmE**
aluminium **BrE** – aluminum **AmE**

2 (20.1) What kinds of materials do they use to make body implants, like artificial hips and knees? Listen and find out.

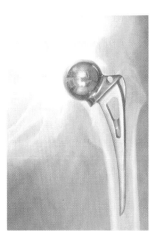

3 (20.1) Listen again and make notes in the table.

	Advantages	Disadvantages
Steel		
Nickel		
Titanium		

4 Match these adjectives to their meanings.

1 artificial	a not hard or firm
2 soft	b able to last a long time
3 ductile	c weakened or destroyed by chemical action, for example, rusty
4 durable	d easily broken, cracks easily
5 brittle	e not natural, made by people
6 corroded	f flexible, can bend repeatedly without breaking

5 What are these things and what are they made of? Which ones have the qualities in **4**?

Think of more adjectives to describe them. Use a dictionary for help if necessary.

6 Which materials in **5** are:

1 transparent?
2 absorbent?
3 flexible?
4 impermeable?
5 porous?
6 natural?
7 good electrical conductors?
8 good heat insulators?

7 Which materials are most practical for making these things and why? And which materials are impractical and why?

1 windows
2 tables
3 roof tiles
4 electric cables
5 bridges
6 shirts

8 Work with a partner.

A

You are going to work on a project in Finland for three months. It will be winter and very cold. You are deciding what to take with you. Ask your partner for advice. Should you take:

1 cotton or woollen vests?
2 woollen or synthetic socks?
3 leather gloves with fur lining or synthetic ski gloves?
4 sunglasses with polarized lenses or plastic snow goggles?
5 wooden or plastic skis?
6 tin or ceramic plates?
7 polystyrene or plastic cups?
8 a torch with a supply of lead batteries or a torch with a supply of nickel-cadmium batteries?
9 wax-coated waterproof matches or a refillable, plastic lighter?
10 a plastic or a steel snow shovel?
11 a pair of rubber boots or a pair of leather mountain boots?
12 a synthetic sleeping bag or a sleeping bag filled with very soft feathers?

What other things should you take?

B

You are going to work on a project in Africa for three months. It will be very hot in the daytime and you are deciding what to take with you. Ask your partner for advice. Should you take:

1 silk or synthetic shirts?
2 polyester or cotton underwear?
3 a straw sunhat or a cotton baseball cap?
4 a compass or a battery-powered global positioning system?
5 a pair of rubber beach sandals or cotton boots?
6 a pair of polarized sunglasses or sand goggles?
7 aluminium or plastic containers to transport large quantities of water?
8 glass or leather bottles to carry small quantities of water?
9 steel or polystyrene boxes to store food?
10 a canvas or synthetic tent?
11 a foam mattress or a plastic air-bed to sleep on?
12 a convertible sports car with a soft PVC roof that you can roll down or a motorbike?

What other things should you take?

Predictions

1 What do you know about nanotechnology?

1 How will manufacturing processes change in the future?
2 What can we build with nanotechnology today and what will we be able to build in the future?
3 How do you think nanotechnology will affect cars, computers, medicines, etc?

Nanotechnology

Nanotechnology is the science of building tiny things. Today we usually make things by shaping materials – cutting, grinding, milling, etc. But in the future, we'll be able to work on a smaller scale and build things atom by atom.

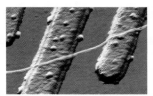

Nanowire (blue) on platinum electrodes (yellow)
Magnification: x 120,000

Today scientists can build nanowires – extremely strong tubes that are just four atoms wide. And when they have the manufacturing systems, they'll be able to build anything we want – diamonds, water, food, robots, etc. We'll be able to make all kinds of things smaller, lighter, cheaper, stronger, and smarter.

We're at the start of a technological revolution and nanotechnology will affect every part of our lives – cars, computers, medicine, energy supplies, food, buildings, clothes. And it will happen sooner than most people think. By 2010 you won't be able to count the number of businesses using nanotechnology.

can and be able to

Be able to often has the same meaning as *can*.
Some scientists **can / are able to** *make wires just four atoms wide.*
Use *can* to talk about the skills people have now.
Use *be able to* to talk about future possibilities.
We **can** *produce nanowire.* (today)
We'll **be able to** *produce nanorobots.* (in the future)

2 Complete these predictions about nanotechnology. Use each verb in the list once.

construct	remove	store	wear
replace	resist	take	send
clean up	perform	stop	

CARS Manufacturers will be able to <u>construct</u> cars from lightweight materials that are 50 times stronger than steel. Today's two-tonne Cadillac could weigh only 50 kg in the future.
The materials used to build cars will be able to ....[1] scratches, dents, and rust.

COMPUTERS We'll be able to ....[2] trillions of bytes of information in a structure the size of a sugar cube.

MEDICINE Doctors will be able to ....[3] broken human bones with artificial bones made with nanotechnology.
Nanorobots will be able to ....[4] surgery.
We'll be able to ....[5] pills containing nanorobots.

THE ENVIRONMENT We'll be able to ....[6] nanorobots up into space to rebuild the ozone layer. Other nanorobots will be able to ....[7] pollutants from water and ....[8] oil spills.

CLOTHES Everyone will be able to ....[9] computers and colour screens because they will be built into their clothes.
We'll be able to ....[10] our clothes from getting dirty by making them with stain repellent fabrics.

3 Discuss these questions.

1 Which predictions in **2** do you find most interesting? Why?
2 Can you see any applications for nanotechnology in your job? What things would you like to be smaller, stronger, etc?
3 Could nanotechnology affect employment in your industry? (How?)
4 Do you like the idea of having nanorobots inside your body? Some people say we'll be able to live for ever with nanotechnology. Would you like to?
5 Is nanotechnology always going to be a good thing? Can you see any dangers?

Possibilities

1 Do your customers ever ask for things you can't provide, for example, special product features, faster delivery times? What do they want?

2 Listen to a customer asking a supplier about a part. What part is it? What does the customer want?

3 Listen again. Complete the questions the customer asks.

1 Can you .... it .... to €30?
2 Is it possible to make them in ....?
3 And will they be able to .... high temperatures?
4 Will they be all right at .... °C?
5 What about ....?

What were the supplier's answers? How certain were they?

Degrees of certainty
impossible
↓
a *It can't be done*
b *Probably not*
c *Maybe*
d *I think so*
e *I'm sure it is*
↓
possible

4 What degree of certainty do these expressions indicate? Are they a, b, c, d, or e?

1 Probably
2 Not a hope
3 Possibly
4 I don't think so
5 Yes, we've done it before

5 Is it possible to invent these things? How certain are you? Write a, b, c, d, or e.

1 a car that is powered by water
2 a device that drives our cars for us
3 a device that stops people from drinking and driving
4 a solar-powered airplane
5 something that detects spam emails and deletes them with 100 per cent accuracy
6 a way to eat more food without getting fatter
7 white paint that stays white and doesn't darken with age
8 a way to distribute electricity to homes and factories without using wires or cables
9 a way to forecast next month's weather with 99 per cent accuracy
10 a device that translates what you say in your language and immediately says it in English
11 something that tells us what animals are thinking
12 a cure for all cancers
13 a computer that's more intelligent than a human
14 a machine that transports us through time

Compare your ideas with some other students. See if you can get them to agree with you.

21 How come?

Explaining why

1 What happens to water if you:

   1 reduce its temperature to 0 °C?
   2 raise its temperature to 100 °C?

2 (21.1) Listen to another question about water. What's the question and what's the answer?

3 (21.1) Are these sentences true or false? Correct the ones that are wrong. Then listen again to check your answers.

   1 Tom's calling because he and his wife have been disagreeing.
   2 Tom's question is: Can you boil water by heating it?
   3 Dr Carter's answer is 'Yes'.
   4 You can boil water by removing heat, or by reducing the pressure.
   5 If you increase the air pressure, water boils faster.
   6 If you increase the air pressure, the boiling point rises.
   7 Reducing the air pressure is a good way to cook spaghetti.

Explaining causes and effects

if	*If you reduce the air pressure, water boils faster.*
make	*Reducing the pressure **makes** the boiling point drop.*
so	*The pressure goes down, **so** the boiling point drops.*
mean	*Higher pressure **means** a higher boiling point.*
that's why	***That's why** you can cook food faster under pressure.*
because	*You can cook food faster **because** the water is hotter.*

4 Explain the answers to some more science questions. First read the questions and see if you can answer them. Then match the beginnings and endings of the sentences to explain why.

What happens if you put an egg in a jar of vinegar and leave it for three weeks?

   1 If you put an egg inside a jar of vinegar …
   2 The vinegar makes …
   3 The vinegar contains $C_2H_4O_2$ …
   4 That means it eats away …
   5 So the shell dissolves because of …
   6 But it's a very weak acid and that's why …

   a so it's acidic.
   b it takes three weeks.
   c at the shell.
   d the shell dissolve.
   e the egg shell slowly disappears.
   f the acid in the vinegar.

Is the earth's North Pole a magnetic north pole, or a magnetic south pole?

   1 If you allow a magnet to rotate freely …
   2 The earth's magnetic field makes …
   3 So the magnet points towards …
   4 But this means the north pole …
   5 This is because opposite poles attract and …
   6 So the earth's magnetic south pole is in the north …

   a the magnet point 'north'.
   b similar poles repel or push apart.
   c it acts like a compass.
   d and that's why magnets point north.
   e is really a magnetic south pole.
   f the earth's geographic north pole.

5 Here are some more science questions. What are the
answers? Discuss them with some other students.

a raisin = a dried grape

① What happens
to a balloon filled
with helium if you
let go of it? Why?

② What happens if
you have a football
in your car and you
stop the car
suddenly? Which
direction does the
ball roll, and why?

③ What happens if
you have a balloon
filled with helium in
your car and you
stop the car
suddenly? Which
direction does the
balloon move, and
why?

④ What happens if
you drop a raisin*
into a glass of
champagne? Why?

⑤ What happens if
you put a frog inside
a very powerful
magnet? Why?

6 Choose the correct word.

① The balloon rises upwards *why/because* the air
above the balloon is lighter and less dense.*

② The ball is heavier, and denser* than the air in
the car. A sudden stop *make/makes* the ball roll
towards the front of the car.

③ When the car stops suddenly, the air inside the
car keeps moving forward. That *mean/means* the
air in the front of the car becomes denser than the
air at the back. This increases the pressure on the
front side of the balloon and *make/makes* it move
towards the rear of the car.

④ Bubbles of air collect around the raisin and
make/makes it rise to the top of the glass. When it
reaches the surface, the bubbles escape, so it sinks
back to the bottom again. Then the process starts
again and repeats itself and that's *because/why* the
raisin keeps moving up and down.

⑤ Some materials are diamagnetic. This
mean/means a magnet repels them. Carbon-
graphite, water, protein, DNA, wood, silver, and
gold are all diamagnetic. A frog's body is
diamagnetic *because/why* it contains a lot of water,
protein, and DNA. So if you put a frog inside a
powerful magnet, the magnet repels it, and the frog
rises up into the air.

* If something is dense, it is heavy in relation to its
size. Density is the relationship of weight to volume.

7 Work in pairs or small groups. Think of
another science question to ask the other
students in the class and write it down. Then
take turns to ask your questions. See if any
'experts' in the class can answer them.

Explaining procedures

1 What trick is this? What equipment is needed to perform it?

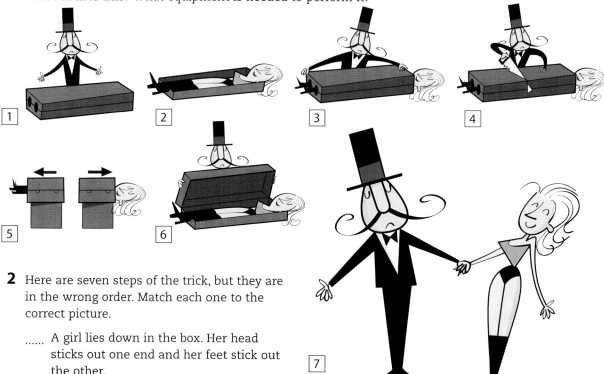

2 Here are seven steps of the trick, but they are in the wrong order. Match each one to the correct picture.

...... A girl lies down in the box. Her head sticks out one end and her feet stick out the other.
...... The two halves of the box are separated.
...... The girl is sawn in half.
...... The audience is shown a long rectangular box with holes at each end.
...... The girl gets out of the box and she's in one piece!
...... The lid is placed on the box and fastened.
...... The two halves are put back together again and the lid is removed.

3 How does the trick work? What step is missing?

4 Here's the missing step. Where does it fit in?

The magician turns the box around so the audience can't see the girl's feet. The girl removes her feet from the holes at the end of the box and replaces them with false feet. She folds up her legs, so the bottom half of the box is empty. The magician turns the box back so the audience can see the false feet.

5 Compare these sentences:

She folds up her legs.
She is sawn in half.

Which one describes:
1 what the girl does?
2 what happens to the girl?

Which sentence is active and which is passive? Complete the rule. Write *passive* and *active* in the correct spaces.

Active and passive

When we're interested in what people or things do, we use .... sentences.
The girl folds up her legs – The focus is on what the girl does.

When we're interested in what is done or what happens to someone or something, we use .... sentences.
The girl is sawn in half – The focus is on what happens to the girl.

6 These sentences say what the magician does. Change the focus and say what happens to the box, the lid, and the audience.

The magician shows the box to the audience →
The audience is shown the box.

The magician:
1 shows the box to the audience
2 places the lid on the box
3 fastens the lid
4 turns the box around
5 saws the box in half
6 separates the two halves of the box
7 puts the box back together again
8 surprises the audience.

7 Complete these descriptions of some more magic tricks. Use the active or passive form of the verb in brackets. (Think about whether you're saying what people do or what happens to them.)

8 How are the tricks in **7** done? (You can check your answers in file 7 on page 103.)

9 Learn how to perform a magic trick and then teach it to another student. Show them how it's done. Different magic tricks can be found in file 4 on page 103, file 10 on page 104, file 19 on page 107, file 34 on page 115, and file 38 on page 117.

10 Take turns performing your magic tricks for the class. Work out how they are done.

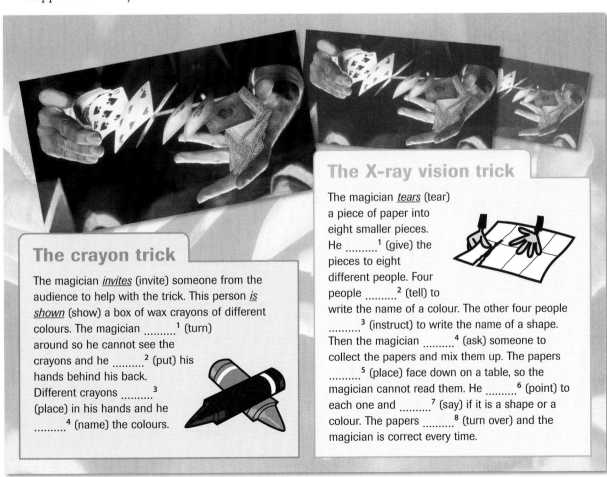

The crayon trick

The magician *invites* (invite) someone from the audience to help with the trick. This person *is shown* (show) a box of wax crayons of different colours. The magician ....¹ (turn) around so he cannot see the crayons and he ....² (put) his hands behind his back. Different crayons ....³ (place) in his hands and he ....⁴ (name) the colours.

The X-ray vision trick

The magician *tears* (tear) a piece of paper into eight smaller pieces. He ....¹ (give) the pieces to eight different people. Four people ....² (tell) to write the name of a colour. The other four people ....³ (instruct) to write the name of a shape. Then the magician ....⁴ (ask) someone to collect the papers and mix them up. The papers ....⁵ (place) face down on a table, so the magician cannot read them. He ....⁶ (point) to each one and ....⁷ (say) if it is a shape or a colour. The papers ....⁸ (turn over) and the magician is correct every time.

Laws of nature

1 Complete the sentences. Use words from the list.

evaporates	stretches	crashes	sinks
dissolves	contracts	bursts	rusts
condenses	freezes	fades	floats
softens	bounces	hardens	ignites
~~expands~~	shrinks	burns	boils

1 When you heat a metal bar, it _expands_ and when you cool it, it ....
2 If you leave an iron bar in water, it ....
3 If you wash jeans in very hot water, the fabric ...., and if you wash them repeatedly, the colour ....
4 Water .... at 0 °C. It .... at 100 °C.
5 Steam .... when it comes into contact with cold glass.
6 If you leave a bowl of water in the hot sun, the water ....
7 Take ice cream out of the freezer five minutes before you want to eat it, so it .... If you don't eat it all, put it back in the freezer and it .... again.
8 A spark from an engine .... the fuel.
9 If you put salt in water and stir, the salt ....
10 If you pull elastic, it ....
11 If you drop a rubber ball, it ....
12 If you overload a computer's processor, it ....
13 If you over-inflate the balloon, it ....
14 The candle .... for three hours and then goes out.
15 If you throw a brick into the river, it ...., but if you throw a rubber ball in the river, it ....

2 Which verbs are connected with changes in:

1 size or shape?
2 colour?
3 chemical state (gas, liquid, solid)?

Which ones suggest damage?

What is it?

1 Read about the dangers of a substance called XXX. What is XXX?

BEWARE OF XXX!

XXX kills hundreds of thousands of people a year and it could kill you.

- Many deaths are caused by accidental inhalation of XXX.
- The solid form of XXX can cause damage to human tissues.
- The gas form of XXX can result in severe burns.
- XXX makes many metals rust and corrode.
- Many electrical failures are caused by XXX.
- XXX causes millions of euros worth of property damage each year.
- XXX can make automobile brakes fail.
- XXX is colourless, odourless, and tasteless, but the dangers of XXX are all around us.
- Acid rain contains XXX.
- Rivers and oceans contain large quantities of XXX.
- XXX is used by nuclear power plants.
- Many people walk miles and miles every day to get XXX because they want to ingest XXX.
- If you don't ingest XXX, you can die.

2 What are the more common terms for:

1 accidental inhalation of XXX?
2 the solid form of XXX?
3 the gas form of XXX?
4 ingest?

The answers are in file 20 on page 107.

Present Perfect

The first picture shows an office before the cleaning and maintenance team arrived. The second picture shows the office now, after they've done their job. Say what the team have done. Use the verbs in the list.

They've picked up the papers.

pick up	clean	wash	fix	replace	stack
turn off	empty	close	fill	roll up	take away

Is it possible?

1 Do you think we'll ever be able to:

1 live 50 per cent longer?
2 clone ourselves?
3 live on Mars?
4 stay in bed and let machines do all the work for us?
5 all speak just one language?
6 stop wars and live together in peace?
7 find an acceptable alternative to fossil fuels (oil, natural gas, coal)?
8 discover the meaning of life?

2 Compare your ideas with some other students. See if you can get them to agree with you.

Information file

File 1

Unit 2, page 8

Spelling things out, 7

B
Call 1
Here is the email address of your sales office: sales@jien-storm.com.jp
A customer calls you.

Call 2
You'd like to look at a supplier's website. Call them and ask for the address. Write it down.

Call 3
There are two people at your company with similar names:
Bettina Maier – email: B_Maier@jvr-tech.de
Bettina Mayer – email: B.Mayer@jvr-tech.de
Someone calls you. Find out who they want to write to and give them the correct email address.

Call 4
You tried to connect to your supplier's website at:
http://www.linx_ware.com/b-to-b.html
but you got a message saying 'The page you are looking for is currently unavailable.'
Perhaps their server is down. Call, ask, and make notes.

File 2

Unit 5, page 23

Explaining what happened, 5

be	give	make	tell
come	go	put	think
do	have	say	use
find	know	see	want
get	look	take	work

File 3

Unit 19, page 89

Inventions, 6

B
1 Read the information on some more inventions. Can you guess any of the missing information?
2 Ask your partner questions and complete the missing information.

Example
Who invented the ballpoint pen?

1 The telephone was invented by Alexander Graham Bell in 1876.

2 The ballpoint pen was invented by .... (*who?*) in 1938.

3 Chocolate was invented by the Aztecs in South America over fifteen hundred years ago.

4 Fibre optics were invented .... (*where?*) in 1955.

5 Jeans were invented by Levi Strauss in 1873.

6 The first successful aeroplane* flight was made by the Wright Brothers .... (*when?*)

7 Paper was invented in China around 105.

8 .... (*what?*) were invented by Thomas Sullivan in 1904.

aeroplane **BrE** – airplane **AmE**

File 4

Unit 21, page 99
Explaining procedures, 9

The jumping paper clips trick

Equipment
Two paper clips and a banknote, for example, a 10 euro note.

Instructions
Ask another student to make the two paper clips jump into the air and join together. If they can't, show them how. (If they can, say 'well done' and ask if they can make a ten euro note into a twenty euro note. When they say 'no', say, 'I can't either!')

How it's done

Fold the banknote into a Z-shape. Put the two paper clips over the top edge of two of the folds, as in the picture. Hold the left edge with your left hand and the right edge with your right hand. Then tell everyone to stand back. Pull the ends of the banknote quickly. The paper clips will jump into the air and link together.

File 5

Unit 13, page 63
Getting around, 11

Answer your partner's questions about some more abbreviations.

VAT = value added tax – a tax you pay in the UK when you buy something

ID = identification – an official document that shows who someone is. Usually it has their picture on it

WC = water closet – a room with a toilet

ATM = automatic telling machine – a machine that distributes money

PIN = personal identification number – the number you need to remove money from an ATM

ZIP = a postcode in the USA. In the 1960s ZIP stood for Zoning Improvement Plan, but people can't remember that now.

File 6

Unit 3, page 13
Project planning, 7

Team 1
Your company has been in business for 100 years, and your job is to plan a large party to celebrate. You want all your colleagues, suppliers, and customers to have a good time, but you also want publicity. So you need to do something unusual to get stories in newspapers, trade magazines, and on television if possible. Choose someone to be your secretary and write notes on these things:

What we'll need:

Materials, equipment, and quantities:

Manpower and time:

Estimated costs:

File 7

Unit 21, page 99
Explaining procedures, 8

Possible solutions
The crayon trick: The magician makes dents in the wax crayons before the show. He knows what colours they are because they all feel different.

The X-ray vision trick: The magician tears the paper so the four corner pieces have two straight sides. The other pieces have one straight side. He gives the corner pieces to the people who write the colours. He gives the other pieces to the people who write the shapes.

File 8

Unit 2, page 9
Measurements, 3

Measurements quiz

1 An inch is longer.

2 A yard is shorter.

3 A 200-metre building is taller.

4 100 miles an hour is faster.

5 100 degrees Celsius is hotter.

6 0 degrees Fahrenheit is colder.

7 A kilogram is heavier.

8 A gram is lighter.

9 A one-litre bottle holds more.

10 It depends. A two-tonne truck is heavier than an American two-tonne truck but lighter than a two-ton truck in the old British measurement.

File 9

Unit 16, page 75
Discussing logistics, 9

B

1 Your partner will ask you some questions about your company's supply chain. Answer them.

2 Interview your partner about their company's supply chain. Ask these questions:
   1 What part of your company's supply chain do you work in?
   2 Do you outsource work? What are the good and bad things about this?
   3 How fast is feedback from your sales team given to designers in your company? Can you respond to market trends quickly?
   4 Do you operate in a competitive market? How does your company keep ahead of its competition?
   5 What's the biggest supply chain or logistical problem you have at work?

File 10

Unit 21, page 99
Explaining procedures, 9

The disappearing ink trick

Equipment

A felt tip pen

Instructions

Use the pen to put some ink on the fingernails of your two forefingers (the fingers next to your thumbs). Hold your hands out in front of you, with your forefingers extended. Tell everyone to watch your fingers closely. Quickly lift one hand up behind your ear and bring it down again with your finger extended, but no ink showing. Quickly repeat with the other hand. Then lift the first hand again and bring it back with the ink showing, and repeat with the second hand.

How it's done

When you bring your hands up behind your ears, change fingers, and bring them down with your middle finger extended. Then do it again, and change back to your forefingers. The secret of this trick is to do it fast so the audience doesn't have time to see that the fingers are different.

File 11

Review and Remember 6, page 87
Body parts, 4

1 A bottle has a neck, but no head.

2 A clock has two arms and a face, but no arms or legs.

3 A river has a mouth and a fork, but it cannot eat. The mouth of a river is where it opens into the ocean. A fork can be something you eat with or a place where a road or river divides and goes in different directions.

4 A coin has heads and tails, but no legs. The two sides of a coin are called 'heads' and 'tails'.

5 A ladder has a foot and no head.

File 12

Unit 3, page 13
Project planning, 7

Team 2
You are going to have a 'Bring your child to work' day when employees will bring their children to your workplace to learn about things that happen in your company. Your job is to plan the day so there are safe and interesting activities for the children to do. Choose someone to be your secretary and write notes on these things:

What we'll need:

Materials, equipment, and quantities:

Manpower and time:

Estimated costs:

File 13

Unit 2, page 9
Measurements, 5

B
Ask your partner questions and complete the chart.

Example
How many inches is one centimetre?

   1 cm = ... in
    1 m = 1.09361 yd
    1 m = ... ft
  1 km = 0.62 miles
100 °C = ... °F
    0 °C = 32 °F
   1 kg = ... lb
    1 g = 0.03527 oz
    1 L = ... pints (UK)
    1 L = ... pints (USA)
1 tonne = 1.1023 tons

File 14

Unit 4, page 19
Gadgets, 9

B
Your partner is a secret agent. Find out what they need to do and tell them about the devices in their bag. Work out which ones can help them.

Example
What do you need to do?
Then you need the … because …

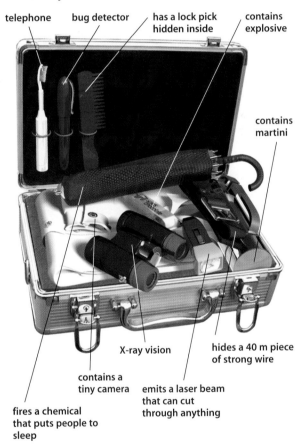

telephone

bug detector

has a lock pick hidden inside

contains explosive

contains martini

X-ray vision

hides a 40 m piece of strong wire

contains a tiny camera

emits a laser beam that can cut through anything

fires a chemical that puts people to sleep

File 15

Unit 7, page 35

Numbers, 7

B

1 Your partner will read some information about the Hoover dam. Make a note of the missing numbers.

> The Colorado River is .... [1] km long. When they were building the Hoover dam, they rerouted the river through tunnels. The tunnels had a total length of .... [2] m and they were over .... [3] m in diameter. They were lined with .... [4] m³ of concrete. The tunnels could carry over .... [5] m³ of water per second.

2 Now read this information to your partner so they can make a note of the numbers.

> They started laying the concrete in June 1933 and finished in May 1935. The dam was built in blocks that varied in size from about 20 m² at the bottom to about 2.3 m² at the top. To set the concrete they laid more than 900 km steel pipe in the concrete and pumped icy water through it. The water came from a refrigeration plant that could produce 907 tonnes of ice a day.

File 16

Unit 5, page 25

Rises and falls, 7

B

1 Listen to your partner's description of their operating costs over the last twelve months. Complete the graph below.

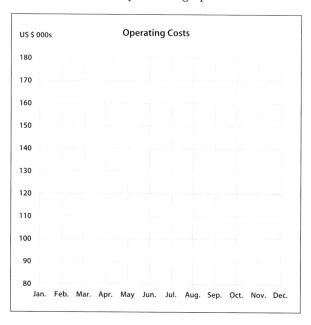

2 This graph shows your company's CO_2 emissions over the last twelve months. Describe it to your partner so they can draw it. Explain the rises and falls.

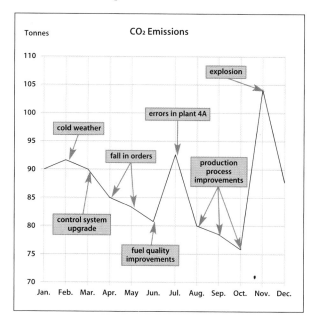

File 17

Unit 3, page 13
Project planning, 7

Team 3

Your job is to create a promotional video of your company's latest product / service. You want to show the sales team and customers how fantastic it is. Choose someone to be your secretary and write notes on these things:

What we'll need:

Materials, equipment, and quantities:

Manpower and time:

Estimated costs:

File 18

Unit 12, page 55
Warnings, 5

Here are the product warnings:
'Do not use snowblower on roof'
'Do not allow children to play in the dishwasher'
A baby buggy: 'Remove child before folding'
Sleeping pills: 'Warning: may cause drowsiness'
Underarm deodorant: 'Caution: do not spray in eyes'
A cartridge for a laser printer: 'Do not eat toner'
'Never iron clothes while they are being worn'
'Never use hairdryer while sleeping'
Wheelbarrow: 'Not intended for highway use'
Birthday cake candles: 'Do NOT use soft wax as earplugs or for any other function that involves insertion into a body cavity'

File 19

Unit 21, page 99
Explaining procedures, 9

The materials trick

Equipment
A pen and lots of small pieces of paper. A container, for example, a glass, cup, bag, or box.

Instructions
Tell the class that your teacher wants to check they know the English names of different materials, for example, steel, wood, rubber. Ask someone to say the name of a material, and write it on a piece of paper. Fold up the paper and put it in the container. Collect names of more materials from other people, and repeat. When you have a lot of names in the container ask someone to shake the container and pick one out. Act as if you're thinking, then tell them what it says.

How it's done
Write the same word on all the pieces of paper. So if the first material someone suggests is 'wood', write the word 'wood' on all the pieces of paper. Act as if you're thinking before you tell them what the paper says.

File 20

Review and Remember 7, page 100
What is it?, 2

XXX is water.

1 Accidental inhalation of XXX = drowning.
2 The solid form of XXX = ice.
3 The gas form of XXX = steam.
4 Ingest = drink.

File 21

Unit 6, page 29

Repairs, 8

B

Describe this picture to your partner. Your
partner has a similar picture, but there are
eleven differences. Find and circle the
differences. Why are the pictures different?

File 22

Numbers, 8

QUIZ RULES

Each team takes turns reading a question and four possible answers. One person from the other team must choose the correct answer. If they're not sure, they can play a '50:50 Joker' and hear the question again with only two answers.

SCORING

Correct answer: 100 points
Correct answer with a joker: 50 points
Incorrect answer: 0 points

Team A

Take turns asking people on the other team these questions. Read the four possible answers too. The correct answer is in **bold** (but don't tell them that until they choose an answer).

QUESTION 1

Roughly speaking, how heavy is the planet Earth?

  60 billion tonnes
  600 billion tonnes
  6 trillion tonnes
  60 trillion tonnes

QUESTION 2

It takes approximately 365 days for the Earth to revolve around the sun. Mercury is the closest planet to the sun. How many days does it take Mercury?

  7   28   52   **88**

QUESTION 3

How many kilobytes are there in a megabyte?

  100
  1,000
  1,000,000
  100,000,000

QUESTION 4

When was the first computer game invented?

  1946   1952   **1962**   1974

QUESTION 5

How much of the air we breathe is oxygen?

  $\dfrac{9}{10}$ $\dfrac{3}{4}$ $\mathbf{\dfrac{1}{5}}$ $\dfrac{1}{8}$

QUESTION 6

Vatican City is the smallest state in the world. How big is it?

  0.44 km²
  3.5 km²
  14 km²
  36 km²

QUESTION 7

The coldest temperature ever recorded on Earth was at Vostok, Antarctica on July 21, 1983. How cold was it?

  –39 °F
  –69 °F
  –95 °F
  –129 °F

QUESTION 8

Some whales can dive to a depth of 2,500 m. What is the pressure at this depth?

  70 bar
  117 bar
  241 bar
  483 bar

QUESTION 9

How much did a litre of petrol cost in Russia in 2003?

  €0.25   €0.75   €1.17   €1.70

QUESTION 10

How much water does an Olympic swimming pool hold?

  1,000 m³
  2,000 m³
  4,000 m³
  6,000 m³

File 23

Unit 14, page 65

Dimensions, 7

B

Ask questions to complete this information. Answer your partner's questions.

Example

How many rail tunnels does the Eurotunnel have?

- 31 miles long
- Has .... rail tunnels and one service tunnel

The Eurotunnel between England and France

- 5,000 years old
- The small stones weigh about .... tons
- The large stones weigh about 50 tons

Stonehenge, England

- 300 m tall
- .... tall with the antennae
- Weighs 7,000 tons (including 40 tons of paint)

The Eiffel Tower, Paris

- .... ft high
- Each side is 751 ft long

The Great Pyramid, Giza, Egypt

- More than .... years old
- Over 6,000 kilometres long
- You can see it from the moon

The Great Wall, China

- 452 m tall
- Two towers. Each tower has .... floors
- Together they have 32,000 windows

The Petronas Towers, Kuala Lumpur, Malaysia

File 24

Unit 10, page 49

Classifying, 8

B

There are no clues to this crossword. Your partner has the words you need and you have the words your partner needs. Make up clues to help your partner. You can't say the missing words, but you can describe them.

¹S	C	I	S	S	O	²R	S		³H			
									⁴O			⁵L
		⁶W	⁷H	E	E	L			S			I
						⁸			E			D
					⁹T	R	U	C	¹⁰K			
											¹¹A
¹²				¹³P	E	¹⁴T	R	O	L		L
	¹⁵										A
								¹⁶			R
¹⁷K	N	I	F	E							M
							¹⁸F	A	N		
¹⁹P	U	L	L	E	Y						

File 25

Unit 16, page 75

Discussing logistics, 9

A

1 Interview your partner about their company's supply chain. Ask these questions:
   1 What part of your company's supply chain do you work in?
   2 Is your production highly automated? Are there tasks that are not automated that should be?
   3 What systems do you have to keep inventories low?
   4 What times are important in your job: just-in-time production, cycle times, lead times, stock turnover times?
   5 What's the biggest supply chain or logistical problem you have at work?

2 Now answer your partner's questions about your company's supply chain.

File 26

Unit 10, page 48
Classifying, 1

Description 2 is correct. It's a battery-free telephone.

File 27

Unit 13, page 61
Giving directions, 7

B
Your partner is at the airport and they need to get to your factory. Their map is old and out of date. It doesn't have the new motorway on it. Your map is up to date. Explain the route so your partner can draw it on their map. (Use the grid boxes to help you.)

File 28

Unit 2, page 8
Spelling things out, 7

A
Call 1
You are trying to email a supplier's sales office at: sales@geinstrom.co.jp. Your messages are being returned. Call the company and check you have the right email address. Make a note of any changes.

Call 2
This is your company's website address:
http://www.eazytek_solutions.co.uk
A supplier calls you.

Call 3
You want the email address of someone called Bettina Mayer. Call the company she works for and find out what her email address is. Write it down.

Call 4
Your computer server is working fine. You have a new online link to your products at:
http://www.links-ware.com/b2b.html. A supplier calls you.

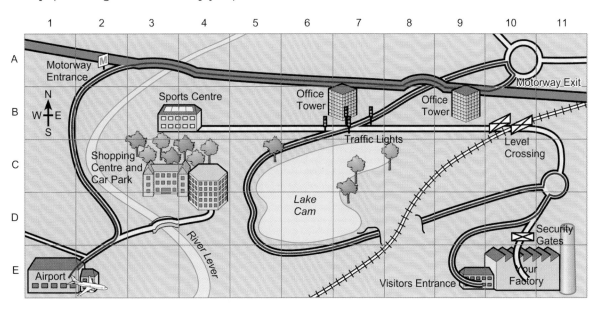

File 29

Unit 15, page 69

Making arrangements, 7

A

Your partner is your colleague. You're working together to organize a web conference on March 12th. Before then, you need to have these meetings.

1 A planning meeting with the presenter (this will take four hours).
2 A meeting with IT to discuss equipment (IT want an afternoon meeting).
3 A budget meeting with the management team (this will take two hours).
4 A practice (you won't have the equipment to do this until March 9th).

Here's your diary* for the next two weeks. You can't cancel or change any of your engagements. Your partner has a different diary. Call your partner and schedule the four meetings.

diary **BrE** – calendar **AmE**

File 30

Unit 3, page 13

Project planning, 7

Team 4

Your job is to rob a bank. You want to escape with as much money as possible. Choose someone to be your secretary and write notes on these things:

What we'll need:

Materials, equipment, and quantities:

Manpower and time:

Estimated costs:

March

Mon 1st	Tue 2nd	Wed 3rd	Thur 4th	Fri 5th
1pm– 5pm Safety Training	9am– 12am Job interviews			9am– 1pm Customer care meeting
Mon 8th	Tue 9th	Wed 10th	Thur 11th	Fri 12th
2pm–5pm: System maintenance		2pm–4pm: CRM conference call		9am–10am: Web Conference

File 31

Unit 7, page 35

Numbers, 8

QUIZ RULES

Each team takes turns reading a question and four possible answers. One person from the other team must choose the correct answer. If they're not sure, they can play a '50:50 Joker' and hear the question again with only two answers.

SCORING

Correct answer: 100 points
Correct answer with a joker: 50 points
Incorrect answer: 0 points

Team B

Take turns asking people on the other team these questions. Read the four possible answers too. The correct answer is in **bold** (but don't tell them that until they choose an answer).

QUESTION 1

The Great Pyramid of Giza weighs about twice as much as the Empire State building. How heavy do you think it is?

- 600,000 tonnes
- **6 million tonnes**
- 60 million tonnes
- 6 billion tonnes

QUESTION 2

How many countries are there on the continent of Africa?

    13   30   **53**   65

QUESTION 3

How many bricks are there in the Empire State Building?

- 1,000
- 1,000,000
- 1,000,000,000
- **10,000,000,000**

QUESTION 4

When was the Eiffel Tower built?

   1792   **1891**   1914   1940

QUESTION 5

How much of the surface of the Earth is covered in water?

$$\frac{1}{3} \qquad \frac{2}{5} \qquad \frac{5}{8} \qquad \mathbf{\frac{7}{10}}$$

QUESTION 6

How big is a standard soccer pitch?

- 6000 m^2
- **7140 m^2**
- 9250 m^2
- 11,320 m^2

QUESTION 7

What is the melting point of gold?

- 962 °C
- **1,064 °C**
- 1,947 °C
- 2,807 °C

QUESTION 8

The heart pumps blood around our bodies. What pressure does it pump it at?

- **1.24 bar**
- 18 bar
- 80 bar
- 120 bar

QUESTION 9

A megabyte of computer memory cost about $5,000 in 1977. How much did it cost in 2000?

- **$0.35**
- $1.15
- $2.50
- $5.00

QUESTION 10

How much water flows over the Niagara Falls in an hour?

- 1,000,000 m^3
- 10,000,000 m^3
- **100,000,000 m^3**
- 1,000,000,000 m^3

File 32

Unit 17, page 79

Attachments, 8

B

You and your partner have the same picture, but they are incomplete.

1 Tell your partner how some things are attached, supported, etc., so they can draw the attachments on their picture.
2 Ask your partner how these things are connected, linked, etc., and draw the attachments on your picture.
   1 the clothes
   2 the bookshelf
   3 the shelf for the teapot
   4 the flowerpot
   5 the ladder

File 33

Unit 2, page 11

Defects, 8

B
Call 1

You bought this filing cabinet from your partner last week. There are some problems with it. Call your partner and explain what's wrong.

You ordered black

Key doesn't fit

One wheel missing

Call 2

You know there were some quality problems at your factory last week. You sold your partner this printer cable, ink cartridge, and web cam. They call you to complain.

1 Find out what's wrong with them.
2 Make notes to give to your quality department.

File 34

Unit 21, page 99

Explaining procedures, 9

The talking coins trick

Equipment
Four coins

Instructions
Explain that you can read minds and ask another student to help you. Lay the four coins on a table and turn around so you can't see. Tell your helper to pick up one of the coins, and hold it tightly. You are going to tell them which coin they selected.

How it's done
This trick requires your helper to hold the coin for as long as possible. Ask them lots of questions, for example, 'Are you holding the coin tightly? Are you thinking of the coin?' Act as if you're thinking hard and having a problem. After  you have silently counted to thirty slowly in your head, ask your helper to put the coin back in its original position. Turn around and complain that your helper didn't think hard enough. Say 'Perhaps the coins will talk to me'. Pick the coins up one by one and hold them to your ear. One coin will be warmer than the others because your helper was holding it. Say 'Yes, this coin says it's the one!'

File 35

Unit 17, page 81

Locating parts, 7

B

This diagram shows an ice-making machine, but five of the part names are missing. Your partner has the same diagram. Find out the names of the missing parts and write them down.

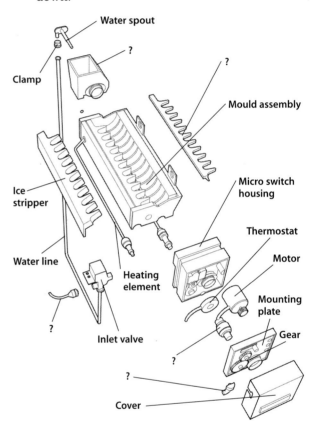

File 36

Unit 19, page 91

Progress updates, 5

B

1 Your partner is your supervisor. He / She gave you this list of jobs to do last Monday. Read the jobs and get ready to tell your partner what you have done.

JOB	
1 Fix energy saving lamp in reception	*Monday 11 am. Replaced transformer – still didn't work. Ordered new power supply unit. Waiting for delivery.*
2 Investigate the complaint about heating system in Workshop 6B	*Installed new thermostat. Job completed Monday 4pm*
3 Replace damaged safety guard on milling machine in Workshop 2	*Tuesday 9.30 am. Someone ordered the wrong part! Waiting for delivery of new part.*
4 Inspect high voltage cable in Workshop 6B	*Thursday 2.30pm. Fixed minor damage to the insulation and wall.*
5 Rewire the plug on the production manager's desk lamp	*Completed Wednesday 4pm. Easy!*

2 Answer your partner's questions and tell them about your progress.
3 Now change roles. You are the supervisor. Last Monday, you gave your partner this list of jobs to do. You want to know about your partner's progress. Read the list and prepare questions to ask.

Examples
Have you checked / investigated / fixed the …?
What was wrong with it / them?

JOB	
1 Check the air tools	*Think something's wrong with the air supply.*
2 Find out why the grinding machine is making a funny noise	
3 Repair the leaking pipe in Workshop 4A	*Urgent! The plant manager complained on Wednesday that this still wasn't done.*
4 Check the oil and air filters on compressor A-96	
5 The showerhead in my apartment is blocked. Please look at it if you get time.	*Cindy complained about it again this morning.*

4 Ask your partner about their progress. Find out if there are any problems.

File 37

Unit 15, page 69

Making arrangements, 7

B

Your partner is your colleague. You're working together to organize a web conference on March 12th. Before then, you need to have these meetings.

1 A planning meeting with the presenter (the presenter is on holiday until March 4th).
2 A meeting with IT to discuss equipment (this will take two hours).
3 A budget meeting with the management team (the management team are only available on Tuesdays and Fridays).
4 A practice (this will take four hours).

Here's your diary* for the next two weeks. You can't cancel or change any of your engagements. Your partner has a different diary. Call your partner and schedule the four meetings.

diary **BrE** – calendar **AmE**

File 38

Unit 21, page 99

Explaining procedures, 9

The moving paper trick

Equipment
A piece of paper and an object that stands upright or vertically, for example, a drink can or a bottle of water.

Instructions
Ask another student to take the object off the paper. Explain they must not touch the object and the object must not fall over.

How it's done
Start at one edge and begin rolling the paper. When you reach the object, the roll of paper will push it off the paper.

March

Mon 1st	Tue 2nd	Wed 3rd	Thur 4th	Fri 5th
	1 p.m. – 5 p.m. TQM meeting		2 p.m. – 4 p.m. Conference call	
Mon 8th	**Tue 9th**	**Wed 10th**	**Thur 11th**	**Fri 12th**
	1 p.m. – 5 p.m. Performance reviews	9.30 – 12.00: English Training	1 p.m. – 5 p.m.: Half day holiday (Take kids to zoo)	9.00 – 10.00 a.m. Web conference

Irregular verbs

Present	Past	Past Participle	Present	Past	Past Participle
be	was / were	been	lie	lay	lain
become	became	become	lose	lost	lost
begin	began	begun	make	made	made
break	broke	broken	mean	meant	meant
bring	brought	brought	meet	met	met
build	built	built	pay	paid	paid
buy	bought	bought	put	put	put
catch	caught	caught	quit	quit	quit
choose	chose	chosen	read	read	read
come	came	come	ride	rode	ridden
cost	cost	cost	ring	rang	rung
cut	cut	cut	rise	rose	risen
deal	dealt	dealt	run	ran	run
do	did	done	saw	sawed	sawn
draw	drew	drawn	say	said	said
drink	drank	drunk	see	saw	seen
drive	drove	driven	sell	sold	sold
eat	ate	eaten	send	sent	sent
fall	fell	fallen	set	set	set
feed	fed	fed	shake	shook	shaken
feel	felt	felt	shoot	shot	shot
find	found	found	show	showed	shown
fly	flew	flown	shut	shut	shut
forbid	forbade	forbidden	sit	sat	sat
forget	forgot	forgotten	sleep	slept	slept
freeze	froze	frozen	speak	spoke	spoken
get	got	got (gotten AmE)	spend	spent	spent
			split	split	split
give	gave	given	spread	spread	spread
go	went	gone	stand	stood	stood
grow	grew	grown	steal	stole	stolen
hang	hung	hung	stick	stuck	stuck
have	had	had	take	took	taken
hear	heard	heard	teach	taught	taught
hide	hid	hidden	tear	tore	torn
hit	hit	hit	tell	told	told
hold	held	held	think	thought	thought
hurt	hurt	hurt	throw	threw	thrown
keep	kept	kept	understand	understood	understood
know	knew	known	wear	wore	worn
lay	lay	laid	write	wrote	written
lead	led	led			
learn	learnt	learnt			
leave	left	left			
lend	lent	lent			
let	let	let			

Listening script

1.1

1 A So how's it going?
   B Fine, just fine.
   A Good meeting?
   C Yes, very good. I think we've managed to cover everything.
   B Yes, we're finished.
   A Good.
   C Marcus has a plane to catch, Elsa.
   B Yes, I'm afraid I must be leaving. Thank you very much for having me.
   C It was a pleasure.
   A Yes, thank you for coming.

2 A You must be Juan Gimez. I'm Sally Thomas. Welcome to BTC.
   B Thanks. Nice to meet you, Ms Thomas.
   A Call me Sally. Did you have any trouble finding us?
   B No, your directions were excellent, thanks.
   A The meeting starts at ten o'clock, so would you like a cup of coffee first?
   B Yes, please.
   A Black, white?
   B Black with no sugar. And can I use the men's room?
   A Yes, of course.

3 A Can I see some ID?
   B I'm sorry, but I left my passport in my hotel room.
   A Do you have any other kind of identification?
   B I've got a credit card. Is that any good?
   A I'm afraid not.
   B Ah – I have my driver's licence.
   A Does it have your picture on it?
   B Yes.
   A That's all right then. Could you fill in this form?
   B Of course. Do you have a pen?

4 A Can I use your phone?
   B Yes, go ahead.
   A I just need to call a taxi.
   B Where are you going? To the station?
   A Yes.
   B Do you want me to give you a lift?
   A Could you? That's very kind of you.
   B You're welcome.

5 A Hi, I'm here to see Mieke van Dam.
   B Could I have your name, please?
   A Gerard Fontaine.
   B Press the green button and the door will open. Our office is on the third floor.
   A Is there a lift?
   B No. The stairs are on the right.
   A I'm afraid I have three big boxes to bring up. Can somebody give me a hand?
   B OK, I'll send someone down.
   A Thanks a lot.

2.1

A Vance Engines.
M Can you connect me with the machine shop, please?
A Certainly.
B Machine shop.
M Hi, this is Martine. Is George there?
B It's very noisy here. Can you speak up?
M Can I speak to George?
B I'm afraid he's out on a job.
M Then I'll email him. Can you give me his email address?
B Yes, it's … are you ready?
M No. Just a second, I need to open a file … OK, go ahead.
B It's g dot bahlow at VQE.com.
M How do you spell that? B-A-R-L-O-W?
B No, B-A-H-L-O-W.
M So that's g dot bahlow at VQE dot com, then?
B That's right.
M Thanks a lot.
B You're welcome. Anything else?
M No, that's it, thanks. Bye.
B Bye.

2.2

A kilometre is shorter than a mile. One mile is one point six oh nine kilometres. And a litre is nought point two two British gallons. American gallons are different. One litre is zero point two six four American gallons. But either way, a litre is a lot smaller than a gallon.

2.3

A Mauro Gelli.

B Mauro, it's Franz.

A Hi, Franz, what's up?

B There's a problem with one of the clocks you sent.

A What's that?

B The base is the wrong size.

A Really?

B Yes, the specs say five centimetres and it's eight.

A Oh no.

B It doesn't fit our packaging.

A Send it back, Franz, and I'll give you a credit.

B Thanks, Mauro.

A Not at all. I'm really sorry it happened.

3.1

A Do you want us to do the packing?

B No, we'll do the packing, but can you provide the materials?

A Sure, no problem.

B How many boxes will we need?

A It's hard to say exactly.

B Roughly speaking?

A Around three hundred.

B Will our computer equipment be OK? Some of it's fragile.

A You'll need bubble wrap for that. Do you have any?

B No.

A I'll send you some.

B Can you move everything in one day?

A It depends. How far is your new office?

B About ten miles.

A Then we can do it in a day. We'll use eight men and two trucks.

B Two trucks?

A Yes, it won't fit into one truck.

B How much will it cost?

A Eight men and two trucks for one day ... You're looking at something like three thousand dollars.

B That's OK.

A And the packing materials will be about twenty four hundred.

B So in total, it'll be five thousand four hundred dollars?

A Yes, approximately.

B Hmmm.

3.2

A Tonight on *Car Chat* we're looking at some of the most exciting ways to get around town. Peter test drives the Segway, the personal transporter that knows what you're thinking.

P This is the coolest thing! There are sophisticated sensors in the platform I'm standing on, so I just lean forward and it moves forward. I lean back and it moves back. No accelerator, no brakes, and it's less noisy than a car.

B Is it better than riding a bicycle, Peter?

P Oh yes. It runs on a battery so I don't have to pedal.

A Also on tonight's show – Claire goes for a ride with the inventor of the Carver – a two-seater car that thinks it's a motorbike.

C Wow!

V So did you like it?

C It's amazing! When we went round that bend, the back tilted over 45 degrees.

V It's fun, isn't it?

C Yes, much more fun than a normal car. It felt faster too. Let's go again and this time I want you to tilt it over further.

A And last but not least, Jeremy takes off in the world's first flying car.

J What's the worst thing about driving?

B Traffic.

D The traffic.

E Traffic jams.

J Well, I'm not going to sit in traffic today. This is the Skycar. It isn't as cheap to run as a car, but if there's a traffic jam, it can open its wings and fly into the sky.

A So don't miss the fun. Tune into *Car Chat* – tonight. Seven o'clock. Radio 416.

4.1

A How do you make it work?

B You have to put a pencil in the holder and then you just wait for bad weather.

A Bad weather?

B Yes, when it rains, the bucket fills up with water. The wood is a lever, so if you press down on one end, the other end goes up.

A So the bucket gets heavy, the wood pivots, and it raises the pencil.

B Yes.

A What's that little thing above the pencil?

B A pencil sharpener. When the pencil rises, it fits inside.

A And the wind makes the blades at the top rotate?

B That's right. They turn the gear and it makes the sharpener spin round.

5.1

This is a true story. On July 2 1982, Larry Walters, a 33-year-old North Hollywood truck driver, filled 45 weather balloons with helium and tied them to an aluminum garden chair. Then he put on a parachute and climbed into the chair with lots of supplies, including some water, a pellet gun, a CB radio, an altimeter, and a camera. He planned to fly across the desert.

The chair was attached to the bumper of a friend's car with two ropes. But when his friends cut one of the ropes, the other rope snapped too. Larry shot up into the sky at more than 300 metres per second. It was so fast that his glasses fell off. He climbed quickly to about five kilometres above the ground.

Larry spoke to his friends on his radio. 'I'm floating across Los Angeles Harbour', he said. He wanted to fly to the Rocky Mountains, but the wind took him towards Long Beach Municipal Airport. Two pilots saw Larry and radioed air traffic control. They were all very surprised.

The air was thin three miles above the ground and Larry felt cold and dizzy. He shot some of the balloons with his gun, the chair floated down, and he landed safely.

Back on earth, Larry was famous. He appeared on lots of television shows and people loved him. But the Federal Aviation Administration didn't think it was funny and they wanted to take away his pilot's licence. They couldn't, because he didn't have one.

6.1

1 A Is the paper tray full?
   B Yes.
   A Have you checked the connections?
   B Yes.
   A Is it plugged in?
   B Yes.
   A Is it switched on?
   B Yes.
   A Have you checked the fuse in the plug?
   B Yes.
   A But you can't make copies?
   B No. I've checked everything. There's nothing left.
   A Have you checked the manual?
   B Ah!

2 A Cold air's coming out of the heating vent.
   B What happens when you adjust the thermostat?
   A Nothing. I've tried increasing the temperature but it makes no difference.
   B Have you tried resetting the timer?
   A Where's that?
   B OK. I'll come and have a look at it.
   A How soon can you get here?
   B Tomorrow.
   A But it's freezing here!

3 A My file is missing.
   B Did you save it?
   A Yes.
   B Have you tried running a search?

A Yes, but it's not here.
B That's strange.
A It could be a virus.
B Or it might be a memory problem.
A A virtual-memory problem?
B No, a user-memory problem. You forgot where you put it.

6.2

A Hello.
B Frank, what are you doing?
A I'm running some safety tests.
B Could you come to the conference room right away? We're going crazy here.
A Of course, what's up?
B A meeting's starting in half an hour and the sound system isn't working.
A What's wrong with it?
B One of the speakers is making a funny noise. We think it's a loose connection.
A I can take a look.
B And we need you to fix a microphone too.
A The wireless mike?
B Yes.
A Are the batteries flat?
B No, we just replaced them. And the projector isn't working.
A Perhaps the bulb's burnt out. I'll be right over.
B Thank you, Frank.
A You're welcome.

7.1

1 A Excuse me. Is the mail room still open?
   B No, I'm afraid not.
   A What time do you close, then?
   B Four o'clock on Fridays.
   A But you're still here.
   B I'm just leaving. It's football night.
   A But I've got three urgent letters here.
   B Sorry, but I'm refereeing. We'll be open again at 8.30 on Monday morning.

2 A Busy day on Thursday.
   B Why's that?
   A We're stocktaking – counting all the inventory.
   B How long will it take?
   A At least eight hours.
   B That's a problem. I've got a training course on Thursday.
   A So you won't be here?
   B Not all the time, no. It's a three-hour course.
   A So it doesn't last all day?
   B No, just the morning.
   A You'll have to work twice as fast in the afternoon, then.

3 A What's it like?

B Oh, you'll love it. It's got a fully fitted kitchen with a washing machine, a fridge freezer, a microwave – everything.
A Is there an Internet connection?
B No, but the bedroom's lovely – nice big windows.
A What size is the bed? Is it a king?
B No, it's a double.
A Does it have satellite television?
B No, but you won't want to watch television. You're just ten minutes from the beach.
A How far is the beach?
B You can walk there in ten minutes and it's beautiful.

7.2

A So the dam is an important source of electricity. On average, it generates about four billion kilowatt-hours a year. Now, are there any questions?
B Yes, how much water does it hold?
A A lot! Lake Mead is the man-made lake behind the dam and it holds thirty-five million, three hundred and ninety-six thousand cubic metres of water. The water pressure is twenty-one and a half bar – that's the maximum pressure at the base of the dam.
C How much concrete did they use?
A Two and a half million cubic metres. That's enough to build a large highway from New York to California.
D How many people worked on the project?
A On an average day, there were three and a half thousand, but the maximum number was 5,218. That was in 1934. It was hard work and dangerous too.
E Did anyone die constructing the dam?
A Yes, people fell into the river and there were accidents with heavy equipment and trucks. The biggest problem was falling rocks. Ninety six people were killed in industrial accidents and many more died from heat or cold. Remember we're in the desert here so the temperature can go up to 44 °C.
F How much did they pay the workers?
A The average monthly payroll was a half a million dollars. The crane operators were the most skilled and they earned one dollar and twenty-five cents an hour. But a normal labourer earned 50 cents. It was the time of the Great Depression and the workers were happy to have a job.

8.1

There are two teams of eleven players and it's played on a grass field. The players have some wooden sticks, a wooden bat, and a small, hard, red ball. The players have to hit the ball and try to score 'runs'. The team with the most runs wins. Everyone has to wear white clothes. You don't have to wear a protective helmet or gloves, but many players do. You need to be very patient to play this game because it can last for an afternoon, or even for five days.

8.2

A What do you think?
B I'm not sure. How does it work?
A When someone comes to the door, they pull this string.
B So this is a pivot?
A Yes, and these are pulleys.
B But is there a problem here? Does the hammer move clockwise?
A Oh, you're right. It rotates the wrong way.
B The bell needs moving over to the other side.
A The direction of the hammer head is wrong too. It needs reversing.
B Do we need to put something under it, to stop it falling too far?
A Yes, and perhaps it needs a spring to pull it back.

9.1

1 A Can you come closer to the machine?
B I'm worried about getting too close to the gears.
A You should roll up your sleeves.
B Yes, OK.

2 A You shouldn't leave these boxes here.
B I don't know where else to put them.
A They're in the way. Someone could trip over them and hurt themselves.
B All right, I'll move them.

10.1

1 This is an implement.
It's made of wood, metal, or fibreglass.
It's long, thin, and straight.
It has a long piece of thread with a hook attached to it.
It's the perfect birthday gift for a man who likes to do nothing.
It's for catching fish.

2 This has a very interesting shape.
It's made of phosphate, sugar, and nitrogen bases.
It's an organic chemical.
It's in every cell of our bodies.
Its full name is deoxyribonucleic acid.
It carries genetic information.

3 This is a very useful device.
It's about twelve centimetres long and seven centimetres wide.

It's often attached to a cable.
It has two buttons on top.
It fits under your hand.
It enables you to move your cursor and click on things.

11.1

A So how do you test the fabric?
B We take samples and attach them to metal frames. Then we set fire to them.
A And what do you measure?
B First we see how fast the fabric catches fire. We time it.
A That's the first test?
B Yes. Then we test another sample to see how far the flames spread.
A So that's the second test?
B Yes.
A Then what?
B If the fabric fails that test, we do a third test. We take a larger piece of fabric and see how fast and how far the flames spread.
A Which test is the most important?
B The second one.
A So it's a big problem if the flames spread?
B That's right.

12.1

1 A What we need is a secret camera.
B Yes, it has to be hidden.
C Then why not install this?
A A smoke alarm?
C It looks like a smoke alarm, but it has a camera inside.
A That's a great idea.
B Maybe, but don't forget we have to install the wiring. Can we hide that too?

2 A As soon as you step on the mat, the alarm goes off.
B That'll work.
A It's simple.
B But very effective.
A We could install one in front of all the doors.
B Exactly, it's not expensive.

3 A What do you think of this? You get a five thousand nine hundred milliwatt shock if you try to steal the vehicle.
B It's amazing!
C It's terrible!
A How about getting some for our trucks?
B Yeah, why not!
C That's crazy!

4 A It only takes ten seconds.
B Yes, but will it work?

A Oh yes. Everybody's eyes are different. It's 100 per cent foolproof.
B Hmmm.
A I think we should look into it.
B It's too expensive.

5 A So it's a recording device?
B Yes, you just plug it into the back of the computer and it records everything your employees type.
C It'll save time if someone forgets to save their work.
B And if someone isn't working – like computer games, Internet chatrooms – you'll know.
C Why don't we try it?
A It's interesting, but I don't think our employees will like it.

13.1

A George Thompson.
B George. It's Marta Sanchez here.
A Marta. Where are you?
B I'm trying to get to you but I'm lost. My map doesn't show all the roads.
A So where exactly are you now?
B Well, I'm just outside Gordstone ... near the entrance to a motorway – a really new motorway.
A That's the M81. They've only just built it.
B Right. So, how do I get to you from here?
A OK. You need to get on the motorway and head south.
B South, OK.
A Keep going for five miles or so. You'll go past a castle on the right and then the motorway forks just after that. Take the left-hand fork and go over the railway lines. Then get off the motorway at the next exit. Is that clear?
B Yes, left-hand fork and the next exit off the motorway ...
A You'll come to Bletcham. Turn left at the traffic lights in Bletcham and head towards Boxted. But don't go through Boxted. Turn right just before it. The road is signposted to Caterhill.
B OK.
A Then you'll come to a roundabout. Take the third exit.
B ... the third exit at the roundabout. Is that it?
A Nearly. Take the first road on the left after Crockley. It runs along a river – it's very pretty. Just drive about a mile and you'll see our factory on the left. We're just after the Pizza Hut. You can't miss it!
B OK. I'll call again if I forget that and get lost ...

13.2

1 A Excuse me. This bill says 'tax: six and a half per cent'.
  B Yes, sir.
  A Does that mean it includes service … you know, a tip?
  B No, only tax.
  A OK, I'm going to pay by Visa. Can I add a tip to the bill?
  B Yes, sir. You can add more when I bring you the check to sign.
  A Oh, hang on a second. There's a mistake here.
  B There is?
  A It should be one bottle of wine, not two.
  B I'm sorry. I'll correct it right away.
  A Thanks, and I'll need a receipt.
  B No problem.

2 A Did you pack these bags yourself?
  B Yes, I did.
  A Has anyone given you anything to carry?
  B No.
  A And have you had them with you the whole time since you packed?
  B Sorry? Can you say that again?
  A Have your bags been with you all the time?
  B Yes, they have.
  A Are you carrying any knives or sharp instruments?
  B No.
  A Do you have any electrical items with you?
  B Yes. My mobile phone, a digital camera, my laptop, an electric razor, my toothbrush …

3 A Does this bus go to Heathrow Airport?
  B Yes, central bus station and terminal 4.
  A Sorry, where does it go?
  B Heathrow central bus station and terminal 4.
  A I want to go to terminal 3.
  B Then you get off at the central bus station. Single or return?
  A Single, please.
  B That's eighteen fifty.
  A Sorry, how much was that?
  B Eighteen pounds and fifty pence. Do you have the right money, because we don't carry change?
  A OK. Er, what time will we get there?
  B Depends on the traffic. Hmmm. About half four probably.
  A Sorry?
  B About half past four.
  A Can you tell me when to get off?
  B Yeah, I'll announce it.

4 A Did you say the price was $228?
  B Yes.
  A And will I have to pay extra if I drive more than a certain number of miles?
  B No. It's unlimited mileage.
  A So there's no limit then?
  B No.
  A And what about insurance?
  B It includes third party insurance and the CDW is $400.
  A What's CDW?
  B That's collision damage waiver. If you have a crash and it's your fault, you only have to pay the first $400 for any damage to the car.
  A And if it's not my fault?

14.1

  A So these pictures are the same office?
  B Yes. How many people can you see?
  A Well, there's one person in the first picture and in the second there are three … no, four.
  B That's right, but only one person is really there. The others are in a different place.
  A How is this different to teleconferencing?
  B With this you can see everything in three dimensions, so it feels like you're in the same room.
  A Are they wearing 3D glasses?
  B Yes.
  A There isn't much light. Are there any windows?
  B No, we have to control the light. We still have a little work to do on that, but there's enough light to see what you're doing. We use a lot of cameras and projectors. You can see a few of them on the ceiling.
  A And you project the images on to the empty walls?
  B That's right. That's the best thing about tele-immersion. You don't have to look at things on a small monitor or screen. We can use walls, tables – so we have plenty of space to display information.
  A It's wonderful!

15.1

  A We need to have a planning meeting. When are you free?
  B I'm tied up this week. Next week's better.
  A Are you free next Tuesday?
  B Is that the sixth?
  A Yes.
  B I'm free in the morning.
  A That's good for me too. Shall we meet around ten o'clock?
  B How long do we need?
  A Well, we need to draw up plans for the product demo …
  B Can we finish by twelve?
  A Yes, two hours should be long enough.
  B All right.

A Then we'll need another meeting with the sales team.
B How long will that take? About an hour?
A Yes. How about Thursday the fifteenth at two o'clock?
B I can't make two, but I can manage three.
A OK, let's say three o'clock then. I'll need to check it with the sales manager, but let's make a note of it and we can confirm it later.
B All right. Is that everything, then?
A No, we need to practise the demo.
B I don't think I can. I'm very short of time.
A We have to check everything's working. Are you free on the sixteenth?
B I'm on holiday then. I'm not back until the twenty-sixth.
A But that's the day we're giving the demonstration.
B I know. Sorry.
A We'll have to come in early that day then.
B What time's the demo?
A Nine o'clock. I'll meet you here at six thirty in the morning on the 26th and we'll practise it then.
B Six thirty!
A I'm afraid so.

16.1

1 Everything needs to be in the right place at the right time, and that's my job. I'm a logistics manager. We transport some goods ourselves, and we outsource some work to shipping companies. Our biggest problem is keeping inventories low. We don't want goods sitting in a warehouse doing nothing.

2 I'm a purchaser and it's my job to buy the best raw materials at the best prices. The biggest problem is price. We operate in a very competitive market and we need to keep our costs down.

3 I'm a store manager so I have a lot of contact with our customers. Now customers can be a problem. First they want one thing and then they want another. They're always changing their minds. You have to listen very carefully to identify the market trends.

4 I'm a production manager and I have to make sure everything is made and packed as efficiently as possible. My biggest problem is product cycle times. We have to find ways to speed up the production process and do things faster.

16.2

A What's the first job?
B The air bags. We activate the air bags so they can't blow up by accident. Then we drain all the fluids out of the car.
A Do you throw them away?
B No, we recycle them.
A What do you do next?
B After that we can dismantle the car, piece by piece.
A So you take everything apart?
B Yes, we remove the battery, the wheels, the engine, the windows, and we pull out all the cables …
A What do you do with all the parts?
B It depends. Some things are in good working order and we keep them.
A And the rest?
B We sort all the other parts for recycling. We have a lot of different containers, and we separate all the different materials.
A What about the plastic parts?
B We can recycle most of them.
A And the glass?
B That's more difficult. Car windows are a mixture of glass and plastic and it's expensive to recycle. We sell the material to the construction industry and they use it to build roads.
A I see.
B Finally we're left with the car body.
A That's made of steel?
B Yes, we crush it so it's easy to transport and take it to the shredder. It cuts the metal up into pieces the size of your hand. Then we can melt it down and use it again.
A Is anything left over?
B Just a little mixture of textiles, paint, rust, rubber … We bury it in the ground. But not the tyres.
A Are they too big to bury?
B Yes, and it isn't economical to recycle them. We sell them to the cement industry.
A The cement industry? Why do they need old tyres?
B They burn them.
A So you don't recycle the tyres, but you recycle the energy?
B That's right.

17.1

A So you need some parts?
B Yes.
A Do you know the part numbers?
B I'm afraid not.
A Which model have you got?
B I'm not sure.
A There should be a plate with the model number.
B Is it on the back of the pump?
A No, it's on the left-hand side, near the top.
B Ah, got it. It's 739 slash 28.

A I think that must be the serial number. The model number is under that, near the bottom of the plate somewhere.

B Ah, is it X47?

A Yes, that's it. Now, what parts do you need?

B Well, on the front of the pump, there's a rod that sticks out.

A The shaft, yes.

B OK, the shaft. The shaft passes through a circular part …

A Through the pulley, yes.

B And there's a belt that fits round the pulley.

A Do you need a new belt?

B No, but in front of the pulley there's another circular part.

A That's the flanged hub.

B The flanged hub. OK, I need three screws for that hub.

A No problem. Do you need a new hub too?

B No, just the screws.

A OK, anything else?

B Yes, there's a part that fits into the …

18.1

1 A What are we going to do about the gears?

B The gears? Why, what's the problem?

C It's our supplier.

A They've gone out of business.

B So we don't have the parts we need?

A No.

C We have some plastic gears. We could use those instead.

B Will they last as long?

C I don't know. I can run some tests if you like.

B What do you think?

A We won't meet the specs if we use plastic.

B So we need steel?

A Yes, steel's more durable.

B Then we need to find another supplier.

A And quick.

C OK, I'll look into it.

2 A Is the fuel pump working again?

B Yes, they fixed it.

C It's very unreliable.

B It's old.

C Then we should get rid of it.

A What – throw the pump away?

C Yes – buy a new one.

B We can't. The pump's obsolete.

A We can't replace it.

C Then let's get a new fuel system.

A A whole new system?

B Do we have enough money in the budget for that?

C We've got to do something.

B But we can't afford a new system.

A Is there a cheaper way to solve this? Why does the pump keep breaking down?

B Yes, what's causing the problem?

3 A Do you have the parts list?

B I'm afraid it's not ready yet.

C We're still working on the drawings.

A What's the hold-up?

B It's the software we're using. It's really slow.

C You press a key and then you wait 30 seconds for a response.

A Can we do anything to speed it up?

C If we get another server, it'll help.

B But then someone will have to install the software.

C And maintain it too.

A Is there a simpler way to solve the problem?

B Outsource the drawing work.

A Is that the easiest solution?

C Yes.

A Then let's do it right away.

19.1

A Stefan, have you repaired the drilling machine yet?

B Yes, I have. It's working OK now.

A That's great! What was wrong with it?

B There was a loose connection. I soldered it and it's fine now.

A Thank you. And what about the turning machine?

B One of the gears is damaged.

A Can you fix it?

B Yes, but I need a new part. I ordered it yesterday and it should be here tomorrow.

A Good.

B And your wife called me this morning.

A My wife?

B Yes, she said there's a problem with your kitchen tap.

A That's right. It's leaking.

B She wants me to look at it. I haven't had time today, but I'll call by tomorrow.

A Thanks, Stefan. You're a star.

20.1

A So what are you looking for? Something strong but flexible at the same time, I guess?

B Yes, they can't be brittle.

A They mustn't break under stress.

B Exactly.

A Do you use steel? That's strong.

B You can make body implants from steel, but there's a big problem.

A It's not resistant to corrosion?

B That's right. Even stainless steel will corrode

over time. We need something durable.

A What about nickel? Nickel doesn't corrode.

B Yes, and it's ductile too.

A What does ductile mean?

B You can bend it lots of times and it doesn't break. But the problem with nickel is it's too soft. We make alloys with it though, like nickel cobalt molybdenum.

A So you combine it with harder materials?

B Yes, we do the same with titanium. Titanium is harder than nickel, but very expensive.

A So titanium in alloys too?

B That's right.

20.2

A These steel springs cost about €40, right?

B Yes, that's right.

A What if we buy large quantities? Can you reduce the price?

B To what?

A Can you get it down to €30?

B Probably not.

A OK. Now, these are steel. Is it possible to make them in plastic?

B Oh, yes.

A You're sure?

B Yes, we've done that before.

A And will they be able to withstand high temperatures?

B Maybe. It depends how high.

A Will they be all right at 120 °C?

B I think so. We can run some tests.

A What about 160?

B Not a hope.

A Are you sure?

B Sorry, but it can't be done.

21.1

A And here's our next caller and he's Tom Berkley from Boston, Massachusetts. Tom, you're on *Science Questions*.

B Hi, I have a question about water. I'm calling because I've been having a disagreement with my wife about this, so I'm hoping you can resolve it.

A So you're having a family argument about this question?

B That's right.

A We hope we can help. What's your question, Tom?

B My question is: can you boil water without heating it?

A Well, that's an interesting question. Let's ask our expert – Dr Carter.

C Hi, Tom.

B Hi, Dr Carter.

C Tom, the answer to your question is 'yes'.

A You can boil water without heating it?

C Yes.

A How come?

C The boiling point of water is 100 °C at one atmospheric pressure. That's the average pressure at sea level. But reducing the pressure makes the boiling point drop. So you can boil water by adding heat, or by reducing the pressure.

A So tell us about this disagreement you're having with your wife, Tom.

B Well, I say water boils faster if you reduce the air pressure.

C You're correct about that.

B Exactly. So that means we can cook spaghetti quicker if we reduce the pressure.

A And what does your wife think, Tom?

B She thinks that increasing the pressure makes food cook faster.

C Tom, I have some bad news for you.

B What's that?

C You need to listen to your wife.

B Ha! Really?

C Yes, if you reduce the pressure, the water boils faster. But it doesn't mean the water is hot when it boils. It boils at a lower temperature.

B So she's right?

C I'm afraid so.

A It's a bad way to cook spaghetti, Tom.

C If you increase the pressure, the boiling point rises and that's why the food cooks faster.

A Does that answer your question, Tom?

B Yes, it does. Thank you, Dr Carter.

C Not at all. Nice talking to you, Tom.

A Yes, thank you for calling, Tom.

ACKNOWLEDGEMENTS

The authors would like to express their heartfelt thanks to the many
teachers who have helped in the piloting of these materials. Sadly there are
too many to mention all of them here, but special thanks are due to Ute
Franzen-Waschke, Sally Bosworth Gerome, Jill Wetherall, Sandi Seiler, Jane
Birgé, Lorcán MacCumhaill, Christine Gowdridge and BMW, Erica Willams of
BEST, and Niall Carey and his team at DaimlerChrysler.

Special thanks are also due to: Shireen Nathoo, Anna Gunn, and Maki Ryan.

Illustrations by: Francis Blake/Three in a Box pp13, 17, 20 (pencil sharpener),
40, 60 (building), 70, 71, 79 (bedroom), 87 (monster), 95, 97 (bottom), 114
(bedroom); Edmond Davis/Meiklejohn pp51, 78; Mark Duffin pp82, 83, 84, 85;
Tim Kahane pp10, 15, 20 (machines), 26, 38, 39, 42, 47, 55, 60 (prepositions),
74, 79 (attachments), 86, 87 (objects); Andrew Kerr pp11 (objects with defects,
filing cabinet), 18, 19, 39, 52, 56, 59 (cylinders, warning triangle), 80 (water
pump), 81, 97 (top), 105, 114 (filing cabinet), 115 (ice machine); Bill Ledger/
Just for Laffs pp84, 85 98, 99, 103, 104, 107, 115 (coin trick), 117; Oxford
Desigers and Illustrators pp56. 60 (map), 61 (map), 88, 111; Andrew Pavitt/
The Organisation pp30, 36, 80 (TV); Stephanie Wunderlich/Three in a Box
pp6, 29, 41, 101, 108.

Commissioned photography by: Pierre d'Alancaisez p30 (notice board).

*The publishers would like to thank the following for their permission to reproduce
photographs and other copyright material:* Alamy Images pp4 (architect/Stock
Connection Distribution, engineer/Bill Bachmann, call centre/ImageState),
28 (printing rollers/Mark Sykes), 35 (Navajo Bridge/Beateworks Inc.),
36 (handheld GPS/Leslie Garland Picture Library), 37 (hiker/imagebroker),
43 (injection/Steve Allen), 50 (bunsen burner/sciencephotos), 56 (iris
scanning/Michael Dwyer, revolving door/Westend61, car thief/Peter Dazeley),
76 (rusty car/Apply Pictures, car being crushed/The Photolibrary Wales),
77 (rubbish bins/Lourens Smak); Associated Press Photo Archive p22 (balloon
man); Corbis pp4 (warehouse/Walter Hodges), 65 (Channel Tunnel/Forestier
Yves, Petronas Towers, Kuala Lumpur/Imagemore Co.), 76 (car being
scrapped/Yuriko Nakao/Reuters, old car batteries/Alain Nogues/Sygma),
90 (businessman/Don Mason), 110 (Channel Tunnel/Forestier Yves),
110 (Petronas Towers, Kuala Lumpur/Imagemore Co.); Fiona Hoskin
p62 (querying bill/Fiona Hoskin); Getty Images pp4 (office worker/Stone,
researcher/The Image Bank), 24 (factory/Andy Sacks/Stone, web press/Taxi),
34 (Hoover Dam/Stone), 72 (Aquarius underwater station/NASA/AFP), 76 (car
air bag/Patti McConville/The Image Bank, landfill/Jeff Sherman/Taxi),
90 (lathe/Martin Schreiber/Stone), 92 (hip replacement/The Image Bank),
93 (Namibia/Pete Turner/The Image Bank), 99 (shuffling cards/Archive
Holdings Inc/The Image Bank); Ideo p67 (Dilbert's Ultimate Cubicle); OUP
pp43 (massage/Stockbyte), 47 (St.Pauls, pyramids, chocolates/Photodisc),
65 (Stonehenge, Great wall of China/Photodisc), 65 (Eiffel Tower/Imagesource),
65 (pyramids/Corbis/Digital Stock), 93 (snowy scene/Digital Vision),
110 (Stonehenge, Great wall of China/Photodisc), 110 (Eiffel Tower/
Imagesource), 110 (pyramids/Corbis/Digital Stock); Pierre d'Alancaisez
pp11 (printer cartridge), 21 (identity card), 28 (key and lock, plug with loose
wire, printer), 43 (hands cutting cardboard, spreading glue), 54 (medical
warning, building site sign), 73 (lump of coal), 96 (egg in jar), 114 (printer
cartridge); Punchstock pp11 (web cam/Photodisc), 43 (measuring/Corbis,
laboratory/Photodisc, painting/Stockbyte), 44 (businessmen/Digital Vision),
45 (rusty bicycle/Photodisc, filing/image100), 56 (smoke detector/Digital
Vision), 62 (airport security/Thinkstock, airport check in, businessman
boarding bus /Photodisc, check in/Corbis), 73 (gold bar/Comstock), 76
(conveyor belt/Photodisc), 92 (steel girders/Photodisc), 92 (neon sign/Photodisc),
114 (web cam/Photodisc); Rex Features pp15 (Skycar), 32 (House of Frankenstein
poster); Ronald Grant Archive p18 (The World is not Enough/Eon Productions);
Science Photo Library pp16 (paper can/James King-Holmes), 48 (ring-pull phone/
Volker Steger), 50 (fire safety test/Peter Menzel), 58 (toy safety test/Volker
Steger, memory testing/Philippe Plailly/Eurelios, blood sugar test/Saturn
Stills), 76 (oil recycling/Robert Brook), 94 (electrical wire/Delft University of
Technology), 111 (Christopher Jung/Volker Steger); Segway.com p15 (Segway
HT); UNC-Chapel Hill, Department of Computer Science p66 (tele-immersion
illustrations); US Agricultural Research Service Image Gallery p58 (Don
Barnard/Peggy Greb); VanderBrink p15 (the Carver); Zara UK p75.

Cover images by: Corbis (man in warehouse/Walter Hodges); OUP (fireman,
surveyor, lab technicians/Photodisc), (oil refinery/Corbis), (woman/Stockbyte);
Punchstock (control panel/Brand X Pictures).

Text sources: p54 From www.mlaw.org; p94 From www.williamsinference.com